Teaching Students with Special Needs in the 21st-Century Classroom

SALLY COX MAYBERRY
and
BRENDA BELSON LAZARUS

A SCARECROWEDUCATION BOOK

The Scarecrow Press, Inc.
Lanham, Maryland, and London
2002

A SCARECROWEDUCATION BOOK

Published in the United States of America
by Scarecrow Press, Inc.
A Member of the Rowman & Littlefield Publishing Group
4720 Boston Way, Lanham, Maryland 20706
www.scarecroweducation.com

4 Pleydell Gardens, Folkestone
Kent CT20 2DN, England

British Library Cataloguing in Publication Information Available

Library of Congress Cataloging-in-Publication Data

Mayberry, Sally C. (Sally Cox), 1937–
    Teaching students with special needs in the 21st century classroom /
Sally C. Mayberry & Brenda B. Lazarus.
        p. cm.
    "A ScarecrowEducation Book."
    ISBN 0-8108-4329-3 (cloth : alk. paper)—ISBN 0-8108-4328-5
(pbk. : alk. paper)
    1. Children with disabilities—Education. 2. Inclusive education.
I. Lazarus, Brenda Belson. II. Title.
    LC4015 .M38 2002
    371.9'046—dc21

                                                    2002003074

∞™ The paper used in this publication meets the minimum requirements of
American National Standard for Information Sciences—Permanence of
Paper for Printed Library Materials, ANSI/NISO Z39.48–1992.
Manufactured in the United States of America.

CONTENTS

INTRODUCTION

I nclusion is a word that has many different meanings in the education community today. The inclusive schools movement has been around since the mid-1980s. Discussions on inclusion provoke strong feelings and opinions, many of them differing. Educators and families appear to feel strongly at each extreme, with few holding middle-of-the-road opinions. *Inclusion,* then, appears to be more than a term for the schoolhouse; it entails a way of life whereby all individuals are valued and have a sense of belonging. An inclusive school is quite simply a school where everyone is included.

Classroom teachers have often expressed concern about the brief notification they are given about teaching in inclusive classrooms. Preparation that both answers questions and equips classroom teachers for their new roles is sorely needed. School systems that readily provide that preparation have found that their teachers, once equipped, step out to do a superb job. In other cases, teachers are left to equip themselves. This book is an attempt to assist in that process. The authors, a special educator and an elementary classroom teacher (both now at the university level), provide preparation in their classrooms and school systems to help others reach the goal of full inclusion.

In this book, you will find background information to help create the historical perspective for inclusion. In addition, there will be activities to introduce students to ideas about inclusion. From implementing curriculum change to grading procedures, awareness issues to successful strategies for implementation, topics are included to assist the teacher in setting up a successful inclusive classroom to meet the needs of all students in the twenty-first-century classroom.

BACKGROUND INFORMATION

1

WHAT IS INCLUSION?

Many educators and families have recently questioned the assumption that students with special needs who need additional services are required to receive them in a restrictive setting, for example, a special education classroom. Instead, the basis for educating special needs students in the "least restrictive environment" has moved to including these students in the regular classroom for the majority, if not all, of the school day. The majority of the supports needed for students with disabilities can be provided in the general education classroom. Inclusion represents the philosophy that students with special needs belong in general education classrooms. In addition, it is noted that further routine removal from the classroom is detrimental to the student and additional supports needed should be provided within the classroom. Inclusion means that students with special needs are to be placed in a general education classroom on a full-time basis with their special needs met in that classroom in order to maximize their learning potential.

Inclusion is defined today in many ways, depending on the individual or organization providing the definition. Phrases such as "full inclusion" and "inclusive classroom" frequently appear in educational conversations. These terms usually refer to the major integration of students with special needs into general education classrooms. These terms have now replaced the term *mainstreaming* because *mainstreaming* has generally referred to some students with disabilities being placed in general classrooms on a part-time basis while others were schooled in separate rooms, trailers, or schools.

CHAPTER 1

Some teachers define *inclusion* as all children learning in the same room with the services they need provided to ensure success for all. Others reply that it is important for students with and without disabilities to have opportunities to collaborate and develop friendships. Teachers note the importance of unconditional acceptance of all children, which focuses on what each child can do rather than what each child cannot do.

The services provided for students with special needs in schools continue to expand and change. Conversations among teachers may reveal varying definitions of *inclusion*. For the purpose of clarification, we will use *inclusion* to mean that students with special needs are fully integrated and based in the general education classroom and receive most, if not all, of any additional required services in that classroom.

HISTORICAL PERSPECTIVE AND THE LAWS

Two separate systems of education have been in operation since 1975 when Public Law (PL) 94-142, the Education for All Handicapped Children Act, was passed. This mandatory special education law opened the doors of public school classrooms to many students with disabilities who had previously been in separate schools or institutions or at home. The passage of this historic law helped many students who were otherwise not receiving an appropriate education achieve access to education. The principle of "normalization" guided the development of the federal legislation. Individuals with disabilities are entitled to the same rights and education as those without disabilities. PL 94-142 mandates that students be educated, to the maximum extent appropriate, with their typically developing peers in general education classrooms in their neighborhoods.

Prior to 1975 most students with severe disabilities (cognitive, emotional, sensory, or physical) went to school in separate facilities, away from their general education peers. Most students with mild disabilities were not identified, or, if they were, they were called "slow learners" but did not receive special education services.

In the mid-1970s the movement to bring students with disabilities into general education classrooms became known as "mainstreaming." Students spent part of the day in the special education class and part of the day in the general education class. For students with mild disabilities this usually meant that they were assigned to a "resource room" with a special education teacher. This teacher negotiated time in general education based on the student's individual needs as defined in the Individualized Education Program (IEP). Some students, usually those with more severe disabilities, remained in segregated settings. But, for the most part, the majority of special needs students spent at least a portion of their day in general education settings.

So what is the difference now? In 1986, PL 94-142 was reauthorized as PL 99-457, and the name was changed to the Individuals with Disabilities Education Act (IDEA). *Suddenly,* the emphasis of the law changed from a mandate to serve *handicapped children* to a law protecting the educational rights of *individuals with disabilities.* In 1990, the Americans with Disabilities Act (PL 101-36) was passed. In 1990 and 1997 amendments were made to IDEA, and it is periodically under review by Congress as part of the Elementary and Secondary Education Act (ESEA). Each time the law is reauthorized, provisions are added, changed, or deleted. The 1997 amendments specifically delineate a role for general education teachers. If a general educator is responsible for implementing the IEP goals, the teacher must be included on the IEP team.

Inclusion is not mandated, as such, in IDEA (1997), but there is a legal presumption in favor of including all students in their local school settings. This presumption is based on a portion of the original law that uses the phrase "least restrictive environment" to describe the goal of placement for students with disabilities. Students are to be educated to the maximum extent appropriate with their "nonhandicapped" peers. Prior to the rise of the inclusive education movement in the 1980s, educators used the idea of a continuum of services when making decisions about where to place students with disabilities. The range was from full-time in general education to full-time in a separate facility.

Within the next few years, IDEA will once again go before Congress for reauthorization. The Bush administration set up the President's Commission on Excellence in Special Education on 2 October 2001. The ESEA is currently being reviewed in committee in Washington, D.C. Bills from both houses are attached to the legislation that impact special education provisions, particularly in the area of discipline. Mandatory special education is a dynamic force within the education community and one that is likely to continue to change as the years go by.

RATIONALE
FOR INCLUSION

Many general and special education teachers have asked, "Why are we doing this?" Some teachers feel that it would be better if special education teachers continued to teach in special classrooms or special schools. General educators talk about not being prepared to teach students with disabilities.

One reason inclusion is happening is that special education has had disappointing results. After twenty years of a dual system, researchers have discovered that students with disabilities have not made the kind of progress in their achievement that had been hoped for by those who set up part-time programs such as resource rooms. Little evidence of a need for separate schools has been found. In most instances in which students in special schools or separate classrooms have been compared with their peers in integrated models, those in the general education inclusive setting have shown more growth.

Further, the world itself is an inclusive place. People are different in many ways besides disabilities. Why should schools be any different? Parents began to say that they wanted their children to be among their normal peers in the world after school, so why not start sooner rather than later? People began to talk about a unified system of education. In this model, there would not be a separation between general and special education. The inclusion movement began to gain steam. Parents of students with disabilities, teachers, and administrators all began saying, "Let's start by assuming that all students can be educated in their neighborhood schools with adequate supports being provided at those sites." Sapon-Shevin (1994–95) has argued that we need to maintain a continuum of services but *not* a continuum of placements. Others have said that a student's special education categorical label should not determine placement. Educators need to look at each individual student before making a determination regarding placement. What does this student need to be successful? What is the least restrictive environment the student can be placed in to meet his or her needs? These should be the guiding questions to determine placement.

In some school districts, inclusion has meant an end to the continuum of services that guided special education placement decisions since the 1970s. In this book, we present successful strategies for making inclusion work in twenty-first-century schools.

SPECIFIC DISABILITIES DEFINED

WHAT CHILDREN WITH DISABILITIES WILL BE IN MY ROOM?

Approximately 80 percent of students with disabilities are in the general education setting for more than one-half of their school day (Turnbull et al., 2002). These students have been identified as eligible for special education services under IDEA (PL 105-17, 1997).

The largest group of identified problem areas in special education is speech and language disorders. Students with speech and language disorders have been in general education classrooms throughout the history of services for this group. A speech and language therapist takes the child out of the classroom for therapy for a short time. More recently, speech therapists come into the classroom to provide services, often providing language lessons for the entire class. Very few students in this group need to be in special classrooms.

The next highest incidence of special education is learning disabilities (LD). LD became a special education area under PL 94-142 in 1975 and has been the fastest growing area of special education ever since. About 50 percent of those students identified as needing special education are classified as having some sort of LD. General education teachers will refer the majority of children found eligible for services under the LD category, the emotional/behavioral disorders category, and a category for those with mild mental retardation. Care must be taken to make sure that language or cultural differences do not influence the referral decisions of teachers.

An excellent Internet source for basic information about special education and other disabilities is the website of the National Information Center for Children and Youth with Disabilities (NICHCY): http://www.nichcy.org/disabinf.htm. The following descriptions of the high-incidence areas are adaptations of the NICHY information from PL 101-476, IDEA:

- *Specific learning disability* is a "disorder in one or more of the basic psychological processes involved in understanding or in using spoken or written language, which may manifest itself in an imperfect ability to listen, think, speak, read, write, spell or to do mathematical calculations."
- *Emotional/behavioral disorder* is a "condition exhibiting one or more of the following characteristics over a long period of time and to a marked degree that adversely affects educational performance—(a) an inability to learn that cannot be explained by intellectual, sensory, or health factors; (b) an inability to build or maintain satisfactory interpersonal relationships with peers and teachers; (c) inappropriate types of behavior of feelings under normal circumstances; (d) a general pervasive mood of unhappiness or depression; or (e) a tendency to develop physical symptoms or fears associated with personal or school problems."
- *Mental retardation* "means a significantly sub-average general intellectual functioning existing concurrently with deficits in adaptive behavior and manifested during the developmental period, that adversely affects a child's educational performance."

General intellectual function is typically measured by an intelligence test. Persons with mental retardation usually score at least two standard deviations below the mean on such tests. Adaptive behavior refers to a person's adjustment to everyday life. Difficulties may occur in learning, communication, social, academic, vocational, and independent living skills. Children with mental retardation do learn—but slowly and with difficulty.

Speech and language disorders are problems in communication and related areas such as oral motor function. These delays and disorders range from simple sound substitutions to the inability to understand or use language or use the oral–motor mechanism for functional speech and feeding.

Attention Deficit/Hyperactivity Disorders (AD/HD) is *not* a category of special education under IDEA. However, there are so many cases of AD/HD in the schools that all teachers need to be aware of the symptoms of this condition. AD/HD is a neurobiological disorder. Typically, children with AD/HD have developmentally inappropriate behavior, including poor attention skills, impulsiveness, and hyperactivity. These characteristics are evident before age seven, are chronic, and last at least six months. Students with AD/HD may also experience problems in the areas of social skills and self-esteem. The difficulties associated with AD/HD often affect academic performance to such an extent that the child qualifies for special education under one of the categorical areas, usually learning disabilities or behavior disorders. Students with AD/HD are also eligible for accommodations under Section 504 of the Rehabilitation Act of 1976. Each school has a person responsible for Section 504 accommodations to ensure that children do not fall through the cracks if they fail to qualify for services under IDEA.

On occasion, teachers will be asked to work with students who have sensory disorders (such as hearing loss or deafness, vision impairments or blindness) or physical disabilities (such as spina bifida, a malformation of the spinal cord, cerebral palsy, or muscular dystrophy); or students with other health impairments (such as cancer, HIV, prenatal substance exposure, asthma, juvenile diabetes, or epilepsy) may be members of a general education teacher's class. When this happens, education, resources, and supports should be provided to the student's classroom teacher.

The majority of students with sensory, physical, or health disabilities will have average or above average intelligence and, with the proper accommodations, will require little modification of the curriculum from the general education teacher. Ancillary personnel such as orientation and mobility specialists, audiologists, consultants, physical therapists, or occupational therapists may be assigned to assist the teacher and the student with any special needs related to his or her disability. These services will be specified in the student's IEP and may be delivered either in the classroom or in a separate setting. The following descriptions cover most of these categories:

- *Hearing loss* is an impairment in hearing, whether permanent or fluctuating, that adversely affects a child's educational performance.
- *Deafness* is a hearing impairment that is so severe that the child is impaired in processing linguistic information through hearing, with or without amplification.

- *Low vision* describes individuals who can generally read print, but only by depending on optical aids to enlarge the print. Individuals with low vision may or may not be legally blind.
- *Functionally blind* describes individuals who typically use Braille for efficient reading and writing.
- *Totally blind* describes individuals who receive no meaningful input through the visual sense.
- *Physical disabilities* are defined as *orthopedic impairments* by IDEA. They include impairments caused by congenital anomaly, impairments caused by disease, and impairments from other causes. Examples of congenital anomalies are clubfoot or missing a body part at birth. Cancer, poliomyelitis, and bone tuberculosis are examples of impairments caused by disease. Examples of physical impairments resulting from other causes are cerebral palsy, amputations, and fractures or burns that cause contractures.
- *Other health impairments* is a category that describes students who have limited strength, vitality, or alertness because of chronic or acute health problems such as heart condition, tuberculosis, rheumatic fever, nephritis, asthma, sickle cell anemia, hemophilia, epilepsy, lead poisoning, leukemia, or diabetes, which adversely affect students' educational performance.
- *Autism* is a developmental disability that significantly affects verbal and nonverbal communication and social interaction. It is usually evident by age three. Other characteristics of autism are engaging in repetitive behaviors, stereotypic movements, unusual responses to sensory experiences, and resistance to environmental change.
- *Severe disabilities* are not defined in IDEA. The term *multiple disabilities* is used to mean concomitant impairments (such as mental retardation and blindness, mental retardation and orthopedic impairment), the combination of which causes such severe educational problems that they cannot be accommodated in special education programs for just one of the impairments. Deaf-blindness is *not* included in this category.

Students with severe disabilities are now being included in general education more than they have been in the past. This can be a daunting experience for a teacher. The teacher may not feel prepared to help students with severe mental retardation, autism, or multiple disabilities such as mental retardation and deafness or deaf-blindness or students who are nonverbal. Most teachers will never have a student with a severe disability in the classroom, but if this happens, a great deal of support should be provided for the teacher. Levels of support will be determined at the IEP meeting. Additional services may be requested once the student arrives in the classroom if supports do not seem adequate. Another IEP meeting may be held to obtain the additional services. The parents of the student are often the teacher's best ally in this endeavor. IDEA entitles a student with special education needs to a free and appropriate education with normally achieving peers.

Teachers need to remember that students are children, first and foremost. They should not be intimidated by the labels of their disabilities. When comprehensive information about a student's particular problems is needed, the family can be of great assistance. At other times, teachers will be the ones to educate the families about the disability. This is particularly true for learning disabilities, for the teacher is often the first person to notice this condition. The Internet opens the world of medical and psychological conditions to educators and families who need more information.

DEVELOPING AN INDIVIDUALIZED EDUCATION PROGRAM

IEP stands for Individualized Education Program. The purpose of the IEP is to give each student who is eligible for special education services a specific plan that is designed to assist the student with his or her particular needs and services. The IEP serves as a written contract between the family and the school district. It documents the services that are needed beyond those that are provided in the general education class.

Each student eligible for special education services has an IEP developed by a team of people. The team must include the parent(s) or guardian of the student, at least one general education teacher, an administrator, a member of the school multidisciplinary team (assessment personnel), specialists in the area(s) of suspected need, and, in some instances, the student him- or herself. Every IEP must contain certain basic information by the federal law known as the Individuals with Disabilities Education Act (PL 105-17, 1997). Each IEP must have a statement of the student's present level of instruction. It must have a listing of the long-term goals and short-term objectives that the student should be able to attain in the current year. The individual who is responsible for carrying out each objective must be identified. The IEP must state how each objective is going to be evaluated, by whom, and when it is expected to be accomplished.

When a teacher is asked to be present at an IEP, he or she should bring samples of the student's work from the classroom. The student's report card or grades, anecdotal or discipline records if any exist, and documentation about adaptations and modifications that have been attempted for the student should be included. If more than one teacher works with the student, a written report about the student's progress from the other classes should be prepared for presentation. Other items that may be helpful to the team are attendance records, recent informal or standardized testing results, and any diagnostic information that has been gathered about the student.

Each school district may develop its own forms for IEPs, but the same basic information is required by all the districts in order to receive federal funds for special education programs and services. Schools districts are monitored on a regular basis by the federal government to see that their IEPs are in compliance with existing laws. Teachers should be prepared to explain any curriculum or behavioral interventions used to achieve an IEP objective.

School districts are required to do annual reviews of the progress of each special education student. The IEP is reviewed at a scheduled meeting to which family members are invited. An IEP is valid for one year at the most before it must be reviewed to determine progress.

If the teacher or the family feels that the student's needs are not being met under the terms of the IEP, either party can ask to reconvene the IEP team. When it does, those present reexamine the goals, objectives, and projected timelines for services for the student. The new meeting may result in a change in the IEP and a change in the services provided to the student. In the case of a behavior or discipline incident, the school district may ask for a "manifestation determination" to determine if the behavior displayed was a result of the student's disability. *Manifestation determination* is a term used in IDEA. If it is found that the student's behavior was directly related to his or her disability, then alternative disciplinary measures must be followed by the school district. This may result in a new placement for the student, but educational services may not be suspended. If the student's behavior is not found to be a result of his or her disability, then the normal school disciplinary procedures are enforced. Behavioral concerns are not the only reason to question the appropriateness of the IEP; academic and social concerns may also be raised. The IEP is one of the most powerful procedures to come out of mandatory special education.

MANAGING CHANGE:
STEPPING-STONES

CURRICULUM ADAPTATIONS

There are several general areas of adaptation that are possible for teachers to make when children are unable to keep pace with the majority of the students in a class. Some children will need accommodations in only one or two areas of the curriculum, whereas others may need modifications in almost every aspect of school life.

Teachers may modify instructional methods for the presentation of information and materials. The learning environment itself may be one of the easiest modifications. This includes such things as providing a student with AD/HD with a chair near the teacher, away from windows that might distract, and away from friends who might want to talk and disrupt the class. Various grouping arrangements may be used in the class other than the traditional rows of desks. Students with special needs often benefit from a cooperative learning activity, if it does not stress pencil-and-paper responses. Changes to time and schedule can be very beneficial to students with special needs. Finally, there are adaptations teachers can make to both their assignments and their assessments that may be helpful to students.

WHAT ARE SOME WAYS INSTRUCTIONAL METHODS MAY BE MODIFIED?

Teachers can

- Use cueing systems for students such as advance organizers and post-organizers to let students know what is coming and what they have discussed in class.

- Use mnemonic devices, such as ROY G. BIV (red, orange, yellow, green, blue, indigo, and violet) for the colors of the rainbow, to assist students in remembering information for tests and other classroom applications.
- Use mind maps to graphically display important information.
- Teach students to take notes by mind mapping, which may suit some learning styles.
- Provide copies of notes or overheads used in classroom direct instruction—the teacher can ask a capable student to share copies of his or her notes with one who may need more time for note taking.
- Use Power Point, Inspiration, or other software presentation packages that assist students in seeing relationships among the major concepts and ideas in a lesson or story.
- Use study guides with the entire class as they discuss important concepts and new material—the teacher can use the study guide on the overhead projector while the students follow along with their own copies and fill in blank spaces for their notes.
- Provide supportive lesson plans by having a capable student take notes on NCR paper or other carbon-backed typed paper—notes, that the teacher (or a capable student) has highlighted, can also be given to a student to enhance learning.
- Highlight important concepts with verbal cues, such as "This is the main idea of the chapter," or use color to emphasize important concepts.
- Repeat key material often—students can start the day's lesson with a brief review of the key material from the previous day.
- Plan for hands-on or concrete learning experiences whenever possible to tap into the various learning styles that will be found in every classroom—planning for visual, auditory, tactile, and kinesthetic experiences in all major lessons will assist students with learning difficulties to achieve success.
- Break lessons into smaller segments or blocks.
- Allow the use of tape recorders and electronic devices when needed.
- Provide students with Braille materials or large-print books when needed.
- Use specialized equipment, such as a Sound Field System that focuses and directs the teacher's voice through amplification—this method may prove especially useful for students with AD/HD, as well as those with hearing impairments.
- Provide a sign language interpreter when needed.

WHAT ARE SOME WAYS THE LEARNING ENVIRONMENT CAN BE MODIFIED?

Teachers can do the following:

- Use study carrels to provide a quiet area for students who are distractible or who need a brief separation from classroom reinforcement.
- Seat students with distractible personalities closer to the teacher and away from windows or doors where distractions may be more obvious.
- Use grouping arrangements to accommodate the differing abilities found in the typical classroom. Small groups, peer tutoring, and provision of additional assistance and guidance on specific tasks have all been used successfully. Teachers need to instruct students on how to participate appropriately in groups. Teachers may also need to reinforce expected behaviors, particularly when groups are first formed, to shape desired group performance.
- Use learning centers or stations for either academic or behavior activities. Breaking up the day with varied grouping arrangements is a real boost to students who need to be able to move around the classroom. It is also beneficial for those students who need to have various learning styles tapped.

The well-functioning learning environment also includes effective classroom management techniques. A teacher can do a great deal to accommodate different behavior styles with specific techniques, such as the following:

- Use daily or weekly reporting and collaboration with the parents of children who have special needs in the area of behavior or emotionality.
- Use checklists for students to self-monitor behaviors, goals, and organization strategies.
- Help students organize their materials and assignments through the use of notebooks, folders, or another self-contained unit.
- Use organizers, agendas, or planners with the students to assist them in keeping track of assignments and their due dates and institute a cooperative program with parents to monitor the use of the agenda/planner.
- Use clear routines for students with behavior disorders—having clear rules and being consistent with enforcement of the rules are necessary.

- Give specific times and dates when assignments are due and help students list these in their planners—posting these dates on classroom calendars assists with the general management of the class.

Teachers should also look at the ways that time demands and scheduling can be modified. Students may

- Be given additional time to complete assignments.
- Be given a reduced amount of work, as long as they can demonstrate that they are mastering the concepts required—for example, if twenty vocabulary or spelling words are presented for a week, give a student with learning disabilities five words to master per day: this is more productive than expecting him or her to be able to memorize twenty words for a test on the same day and allows him or her to do it in chunks of five words per day.
- Be allowed to reduce the length of their assignments.
- Be scheduled for a modified class day—for example, students with medically fragile conditions, health impairments, or severe behavior or emotional disabilities may need to come to school for fewer hours each day.
- Be allowed more time to finish a course if necessary—this option would be more commonly used at the secondary school level.
- Thrive in a multiage grouping classroom—this type of classroom may provide a natural setting for making necessary accommodations in time and scheduling for students who need these adaptations.

Teachers should look for ways that classroom assignments and assessments can be modified. Assignments may be modified by

- Students using word processors, recorders, or responding orally to some assignments.
- Avoiding cluttered or crowded worksheets by blocking assignments or cutting the worksheet into segments for students with special needs.
- Using folders or notebooks for storing assignments.
- Students using the appropriate assistive technology.
- Students using alternative modes for presentations, such as oral reports.
- Simulations, model building, or Power Point presentations.

- Allowing students to use manipulative objects as much as possible for concrete, hands-on experiences.
- Having students dictate the first draft of a report to a peer, or the teacher, and then typing the final version.
- Students choosing eight out of ten problems or questions to complete and grading them on those eight problems.

Assessments may be modified by

- Providing prior review or debriefing for students.
- Providing extra time to complete the test for students who need it.
- Dividing the administration of the test over several days if possible.
- Testing students orally or using a tape recorder for directions.
- Allowing students to write directly on the test rather than on answer sheets.
- Having students sit where they are comfortable to take the test.
- Providing snack breaks between segments of the testing.
- Testing differently than the normal presentation—for example, in spelling, instead of always giving dictation tests, provide students with four spellings of a word and allow them to choose the correct spelling of the word.

The teacher needs to be familiar with accommodations that are allowed on state and national assessment tests. Students with special needs may be eligible to receive these accommodations by their IEPs. When teachers in general education classrooms provide simple accommodations for students with special needs, success is possible for these students in the general education classroom.

MULTIPLE
INTELLIGENCES

Gardner's (1983, 1993) theory of multiple intelligences (MI) has generated a great deal of interest. The implementation of MI in classrooms offers teachers an opportunity to meet the needs of all learners in their classrooms. Armstrong (1994) has translated Gardner's theories and put them into practical application for the reality of the classroom for teachers. The theory of MI asks teachers to consider that people learn in various ways and, therefore, may show their intelligence in various ways.

Schools have traditionally rewarded linguistic and logical-mathematical intelligences both in the design of the curriculum and in how intelligence has been assessed. The MI theory is based on the belief that teachers should look at how people solve problems and how they create products in a natural setting (Armstrong, 1994).

Each of the existing multiple intelligences is listed below followed by a key word descriptor and a guiding question that may lead the reader to begin to use MI in curriculum development:

- *Linguistic* (Words): How can I use the spoken or written word?
- *Logical–Mathematical* (Numbers): How can I bring in numbers, calculations, logic, classification, or critical thinking skills?
- *Spatial* (Pictures): How can I use visual aids, visualization, color, art, or metaphor?
- *Bodily–Kinesthetic* (Body): How can I involve the whole body or use hands-on experiences?

- *Musical* (Music): How can I bring in music or environmental sounds or set key points in a rhythmic or melodic framework?
- *Interpersonal* (People): How can I engage students in peer sharing, cooperative learning, or large-group simulation?
- *Intrapersonal* (Self): How can I evoke personal feelings or memories or give students choices?
- *Naturalist* (Nature): How can I bring in environmental, ecological, or natural resources? (Armstrong, 1994)

How can thinking about these varied forms of intelligence help teachers work with students who have disabilities? For too long, educators have looked at the deficits of students with disabilities and not at their strengths. This model can help teachers begin to focus on growth and to look for the positive contributions that can be made when students are given an opportunity to express their intelligence in different ways.

MI theory can help teachers recognize that a student's disability is only one part of that child's life. MI can provide teachers with a means of using the strengths of their students to bypass their weaknesses. Teachers who use this method have found that by providing the best activities for students with disabilities and other special needs, they are reaching all of their students. These strategies work with all types of learners.

MI theory can be used to guide teachers when they are developing IEPs. Teachers can identify the strengths and preferred learning styles of each student under the "Present Level of Performance" section of the IEP and use these to guide the selection of strategies and interventions. IEPs should list interventions designed to take advantage of the students' strengths. When students have the opportunity to work from their strengths, self-esteem begins to build and achievement rises. Thus, a positive trend begins to build.

AUTHENTIC ASSESSMENT

Inclusion requires that teachers make their classrooms, materials, curriculum, activities, and assessment tasks relevant for all students including general education students and those with special needs (Finson, 1996). Proponents of authentic assessment use multiple assessment sources for evaluation purposes while striving to measure student and program success in innovative ways. This form of assessment is an organized effort to obtain information about what each student knows and is able to demonstrate and can be used effectively for all students. Standardized tests are no longer acceptable as the *sole* measure of student progress. Techniques that allow students and teachers to select a variety of ways to illustrate progress toward a goal are coming to the forefront in many school systems.

Effective assessment or evaluation is a continuous process. It is integrated into all areas of the curriculum and provides students and teachers with data to assess and improve student learning and interpret the effectiveness of the materials, instructional strategies, and teaching methodology used within that classroom. A variety of evaluation tools is required to make an accurate assessment of materials, strategies, and learning within the classroom. Authentic assessment is far more than creating a test, administering the test, grading and recording the test, and then returning it to the student.

The use of authentic assessment is an important ingredient in the inclusive classroom. These types of assessment are closely related to the types of individualistic, performance-based assessment tasks long implemented in special education classrooms. Using a variety of authentic assessment types, students are able to construct a best-fit situation for illustrating their learning in a nontraditional manner. In implementing the use of authentic assessment, students are empowered to integrate their learning, utilize higher-level thinking and problem solving, and evaluate their own accomplished goals through reflection and self-assessment. There are numerous types of authentic assessment available for use in the classroom today. Two specific types, performance assessment and portfolio assessment, will be defined here. In conclusion, the development and implementation of rubrics for scoring purposes will be addressed.

PERFORMANCE ASSESSMENT

It is important to implement assessment procedures that are compatible with the classroom instructional objectives and strategies. To teach using hands-on science activities followed by a multiple-choice test sends a confusing message to the students (Finson, 1996). Performance assessment is a hands-on type of assessment that allows the students to demonstrate their knowledge and understanding of an activity, lesson, or unit in the same manner in which they were taught. This demonstration can be shown using manipulatives or hands-on materials in a mathematics or science lesson in which students are presented with a problem and asked to discover a solution using the materials provided. Students are asked to present the rationale for the selection of a particular activity. In this manner, students are given the opportunity to apply their new knowledge rather than to memorize facts for a paper-and-pencil test.

Another version of performance assessment allows the students to prepare an activity that illustrates their new knowledge to their classmates. This might take the form of a creative poem, play, rap, song, quiz show, mock interview with a famous person, poster session, and so on. The product can be an individual or group creation. Students who experienced both this type of performance assessment and the standard memorized quiz strongly voiced their preferences for the performance type of assessment to promote learning over time.

PORTFOLIOS

A portfolio is a collection of evidence that illustrates progress toward a goal, a showcase of student work. The portfolio illustrates far more about student learning than a single test or series of tests (Stenmark, 1991). One of the beauties of portfolios is that each student can select and create a product that illustrates his or her own progress in his or her own creative way. Student portfolios are not compared with one another. A student is measured in progress toward each of his or her own individual goals. The portfolio should be well organized and include self-evaluation and reflection by the student on the chosen artifacts. Portfolios may be used to promote parent involvement in students' education in a meaningful way. They may also serve as a means for discussion between the teacher and individual students about academic strengths and areas for improvement.

RUBRICS

A rubric is a guide to follow when scoring authentic assessments. It provides a detailed breakdown of points to be awarded for the learner's response and specifically how those points may be earned. It is imperative that the rubric be developed prior to the assignment of each task and be shared with each student to promote understanding of the exact requirements. When students become aware of the specific levels of the task prior to completing the task, they are more likely to complete that assignment successfully (Finson, 1996).

In developing a rubric for a performance assessment task or portfolio, the teacher must first determine what items are to be valued. Describe what is expected in three or four groups (the equivalent of three or four different grade or numerical values). In other words, to obtain an A, a science poster presentation should include an accurate depiction of the science experiment in pictures and words, contain correct spelling and grammar, present scientifically correct information, and be explained to the class orally with enthusiasm. Each of these four areas could be assigned one point (or as many points as one cares to designate). Four points would equal an A. If only three areas are covered well, three points would equal a B, and so on. A copy of the rubric (a chart format is recommended) should be given to each student when the assignment is first introduced. Each student can immediately visualize the teacher's expectations for the quality of work required to achieve each specific grade.

The use of authentic assessment in the inclusive elementary classroom allows teachers to more effectively evaluate the progress of each individual student. The gradual implementation of authentic assessment in the form of performance and portfolio assessment is highly recommended.

CONSTRUCTIVIST
LEARNING

Constructivism is defined as a form of active learning in which the students play a major part in their own learning process (Stork and Engel, 1999). The constructivist teacher is responsible for an environment that includes activities, problems, and challenges that encourage the students to create their own knowledge. The constructivist classroom differs considerably from the standard classroom where the teacher is the sole transmitter of knowledge and director of all activities. Instead, in the constructivist classroom, the teacher becomes the facilitator of classroom projects and activities. Students are allowed to choose activities and make decisions about classroom rules and standards.

Most teachers teach as they were taught (Fosnot, 1996). It is important to discover ways in which this cycle can be interrupted. Brooks and Brooks (1993) suggest that teachers must themselves become co-learners with their own students. In order to become a constructivist teacher, one first must become a constructivist learner.

Learning is not just an accumulation of isolated facts. In the constructivist model, learning is the creation of meaning. That meaning is created when the student is empowered to link new knowledge with already existing knowledge. Learners then construct their own knowledge.

Constructivist theory can readily be woven into the inclusive classroom. Constructivism promotes the idea that all students are continuously learning. All students, whether general education or special needs, must be met at their current level. Each student enters the classroom door with different knowledge levels and the abilities to learn in different ways. It is every teacher's responsibility to ensure that new knowledge is related in meaningful ways to each student's current knowledge base without placing the emphasis on constant remediation. The role of the teacher is to empower the students to construct or build "deeper understandings" (Brooks and Brooks, 1993). Teachers should set up learning environments in which students are encouraged to search for meaning while becoming active learners.

There are stumbling blocks evident in the inclusive classroom as well as the general education classroom that frustrate learning and the search for understanding. Some of these stumbling blocks are

- Large time frames of teacher talk.
- A totally textbook-oriented curriculum.
- The devaluation of student thinking.
- Overemphasis on curriculum mastery.
- The lack of cooperative grouping activities.

In opposition to these practices, the following stepping-stones are advocated:

- Encouraging student-to-student and teacher-to-student interaction.
- Providing opportunities for cooperative learning activities.
- Integrating curriculum areas.
- Encouraging students to think and rethink problems and activities.
- Providing students with opportunities to demonstrate and exhibit their knowledge in ways other than the traditional "Friday" test.

National standards encourage the use of problem solving and emphasize the importance of constructing solutions rather than rote memorization. *The Curriculum and Evaluation Standards for School Mathematics* (National Council of Teachers of Mathematics [NCTM], 1989) stresses the use of the constructivist model. The new *Principles and Standards for School Mathematics* (NCTM, 2000) builds and expands on these constructivist ideas, recommending a strong mathematics curriculum, knowledgeable teachers who can integrate instruction and assessment, and a school commitment to excellence. *The National Science Education Standards* (National Research Council, 1995) calls for constructivist reform involving hands-on experiments and learner-generated investigations. In the standards it is recommended that teachers cover less content in the curriculum but cover that content in greater depth.

In order to promote constructivist student-centered learning, a student must perceive the problem posed as one relevant to his or her life. How does a teacher help students perceive a topic or problem to be important and relevant to their world? According to Greenberg,

1. The students first create a prediction which can be tested.
2. The plan should involve the use of inexpensive equipment.
3. The problem should be complex to ensure multiple problem-solving approaches.
4. Group effort is beneficial.
5. The students should perceive the problem as relevant. (in Brooks and Brooks, 1993, p. 36).

In the promotion of the constructivist trend of teaching, five guiding principles should be included:

1. Problems of emerging relevance should be posed to students.
2. Learning should be structured around primary concepts.
3. Students' points of view should be both sought and valued.
4. Curriculum should be adapted to address students' concerns.
5. Student learning should be assessed within the meaningful context of teaching (Brooks and Brooks, 1993, p. 33).

In summary, the constructivist teacher will

- Encourage and accept student thoughts and feedback.
- Use manipulatives, hands-on activities, and cooperative grouping.
- Stretch students' thinking by using wait time and open-ended, thought-provoking questions.
- Continually check on student levels of understanding.
- Seek elaboration and allow process time.

In this manner, teachers can implement the bold changes recommended by the constructivist model to assist students in their search for knowledge and pursuit of understanding.

MANAGING CHANGE:
STUMBLING BLOCKS

INADEQUATE TEACHER PREPARATION

The movement to educate students with disabilities in general education settings has been gaining in acceptance since mandatory special education was passed in 1975 under PL 94-142, now known as the Individuals with Disabilities Education Act (PL 105-17). Although it has been over twenty-five years since this law was passed, there is still a failure to fully realize the possibilities of inclusive classrooms. The slow pace of including all students with disabilities into classrooms has to do, in part, with inadequate teacher education programs.

State requirements for the training of general education teachers have not changed significantly since IDEA was passed. Some preservice programs added a three-hour course in special education or inclusive practices, but the results have been minimal (Lesar et al., 1997).

The broad reforms in teacher education have operated on separate, parallel tracks in general and special education, but they have paved the way for more inclusive teacher education programs (Winn and Blanton, 1997). The culture of higher education in many universities works against the integration of programs. Departments with resource allocations based on enrollment in separate programs have strong political bases in universities (Winn and Blanton, 1997). The very structure of a university, set up with discrete departments, acts as a barrier to inclusive teacher education programs. Students going through a traditional program have not seen collaboration modeled, nor have they been given an opportunity to do collaborative activities in their classes (Ornstein and Behar-Horenstein, 1999). If they go out to the schools without having had any experience in collaborative work, they will most likely perpetuate the separation model.

In recent years there have been a number of university programs that have integrated their elementary and special education programs in models whose names include terms such as *unified* or *integrated* (Sherry and Spooner, 2000). It is too early in their development to determine the success of such approaches, but preliminary results are promising. Requirements for state licensure and university degree requirements make the integration of programs difficult, if not impossible, at the undergraduate level. Many states have set limits on the number of hours required for a baccalaureate degree, and certification programs must stay within those limits (e.g., the state of Florida has a 120-hour maximum credit limit for an undergraduate degree).

On the other hand, the role of the classroom teacher is changing to reflect more collaboration in inclusive settings. Colleges of Education must change with the times, as well, in order to prepare the next generation of educators to meet the challenges of diverse schools. The time is right for change. There are major reforms under way in general education and in teacher education. Several of them mesh well with the implementation of integrated teacher education programs. Examples are

- The new knowledge of teaching and learning in curriculum.
- The provision of opportunities for preservice students to work in diverse settings.
- The establishment of professional development schools.

The standards and accountability movement will also help to push reform in Colleges of Education where reform is slow. For example, for accreditation by the National Council of Associations of Teacher Education, all teacher education program graduates must meet the standard stating that general education students must demonstrate "adapting instruction for culturally diverse and exceptional populations" (Wise, 1994, p. 9).

Integrated teacher education programs have been developed around the country. Most of the existing models have resulted from a restructuring or blending of traditional teacher preparation programs in early childhood, elementary, secondary, and special education. The most popular framework has been the development of a common core of courses that all teacher education students take, regardless of their chosen major. Such a core might include the following types of courses or competencies for all future teachers:

- History and philosophy of education.
- Child and adolescent development.
- Human relations and human differences.
- Classroom organization, management, and motivation strategies.
- Measurement and authentic assessment.
- Peer-mediated strategies (cooperative learning, peer tutoring, group learning, mediation, and conflict resolution).
- Adapting instruction to individual differences.
- Use of audiovisual, media, and computer technology.
- Home, school, and community relations.
- Issues and trends in education.
- Creativity and collaborative teaming (Ornstein and Behar-Horenstein, 1999, p. 59).

The list may appear to be typical of many traditional teacher preparation programs, but a closer inspection does reveal some new trends. These are collaboration, technology, family and community partnerships, and group and individual work. Future teachers should be prepared to go out into the inclusive classrooms of today.

Some of the major findings from educational psychology and teacher education in the past fifteen years have helped to guide teacher educators as they shape new programs. Wigle and Wilcox (1996) have grouped the criteria for the preparation of educational personnel under the following major findings:

- Substantive student–teacher interaction and sufficient field experience prior to student teaching and careful placement with skilled inservice teachers.
- The opportunity to respond, monitoring student learning skills and question-asking skills.
- Academic engaged time, developing the mind-set that all students can grow and learn, not just those students who are more capable, and planning and implementing a greater number of activities and materials to accommodate a variety of learning styles.

- A relevant curriculum, thereby designing learning activities that facilitate academic engagement on the part of all students, especially those with disabilities.
- Maximizing student success, with a thorough understanding of the concept of the least restrictive environment.

How can a classroom teacher have an impact on teacher education? If the way teachers have been prepared in the past is a barrier to inclusive classrooms, then classroom teachers need to find ways to help shape the university program. Several avenues are possible:

1. Professional Development School Involvement: If the school has a strong partnership with a university or is a professional development school (PDS) by formal agreement between the district and the university, teachers have a natural way to get involved. Some of the national teacher education reforms suggest that all practice, internships, and student teaching should be done in PDSs. Teachers at PDSs are often given the opportunity to teach or co-teach on-site seminars or classes.

2. Clinical Supervision of Interns and Student Teachers: Many universities prefer to send preservice teachers to a school in a "cluster." This practice is both economical and pedagogically sound. A university supervisor does not have to spend as much time in a car driving to several different sites. Teachers at the local school have more of an opportunity to give feedback to the university as the supervisor is in the building on a more frequent basis. Collaboration, seminars, and sharing of ideas can all be done at the school.

3. Focus Groups: University faculties often hold focus group sessions to obtain teacher input when changes in their program are being considered. Invitations to these sessions are usually given to recent local graduates of the programs, to teachers who supervise student teachers, and to local administrators. Some states require publication of these meetings in the local newspaper with an open invitation to the community for input.

4. Newspapers: Newspapers are also a source for planned activities at the local college or university. They often feature articles about exciting things that are going on in teacher education in the community. Community

members may contact the dean/director of teacher education at the university to volunteer to assist in the redesign of teacher education.

Why have the university programs been slow to respond to the reforms in public education? The culture of the university, structure of academic departments, reward structure, resource allocation, and academic freedom are real, or perceived, barriers to change. As is the case in PK–12 education, faculty members are rarely rewarded for curriculum development work.

Many colleges and universities have chosen to integrate and reform their teacher education programs in the past ten years despite these barriers. There are models around the country that may be examined (see Blanton et al., 1997; Ornstein and Behar-Horenstein, 1999). A number of teacher education programs have become five-year models after the recommendation of the Holmes Group (1986).

York and Reynolds (1996) have reviewed the research literature on what students in teacher education programs should know related to students with disabilities. Three distinct areas of knowledge have been found. They classify this knowledge as what special educators need to know, what general educators need to know, and what is common knowledge for the two groups of professionals. Although the dichotomy of training may seem to be perpetuated by this division, it is instructive to look at the two lists when considering the components of a unified teacher education program.

Special educators need to know

- The philosophical, historical, and legal foundations of special education.
- Characteristics of learners.
- Assessment, diagnosis, and evaluation.
- Instructional content and practice.
- How to plan and manage the teaching and learning environment.
- How to manage student behavior and social interaction skills.
- Communication and collaborative partnerships.
- Professionalism and ethical practices.

These categories make up the basic education standards of the Council for Exceptional Children (York and Reynolds, 1996). General educators need to have numerous competencies to be effective in inclusive classrooms. Some of these are the following:

- Assess the needs of students and evaluate learning.
- Understand curriculum and use appropriate teaching techniques.
- Establish effective parent–teacher relationships.
- Foster student–student relationships.
- Be knowledgeable about resource and support systems.
- Manage the learning environment.
- Demonstrate competent interpersonal communication.
- Supervise aides and volunteers.
- Understand legal issues.
- Carry out behavior management plans (York and Reynolds, 1996).

Is it possible to combine competencies into a core of knowledge for all future teachers? This is currently being recommended. There is more overlap than difference in the two lists. The curriculum is changing in teacher education to better prepare the next generation of classroom teachers to meet the realities of today's classrooms.

CO-TEACHING

Co-teaching is one of the most powerful developments to come out of the inclusion movement. There are several variations of how co-teaching works, but in its most basic design the practice involves the pairing of two teachers, one a general educator and the other a special educator, to more adequately address the needs of students with disabilities and other at-risk students who may, or may not, be labeled for special assistance. In this arrangement, up to one-third of the students assigned to the co-teachers might be in special education. The class size may be larger than one general education classroom but have fewer students than two classes. There is no pullout from the general education class for the students in special education to go to a separate room with a separate teacher. All instruction, accommodations, and modifications are implemented right in the classroom and are delivered to all students who can benefit from them, whether they are in special education or not.

If co-teaching is to succeed, according to Bos and Vaughn (1998) there are five critical areas that must be addressed by the co-teachers:

- Who will grade, and how will grades be determined?
- What classroom management procedures and classroom rules will be put in place?
- How will the teachers define their own space? Both teachers need storage and working areas that are comparable.

CHAPTER 11

- How will having two teachers in the room be explained to students and parents?
- How will the co-teachers get uninterrupted planning time together each week?

In this model, students are "ours" not "yours or mine." By teaching together the teaching partners learn from each other, and the result is more powerful than the effect of two separate teachers. General educators usually have more knowledge of curriculum and subject areas. Special educators usually have more expertise in the use of learning strategies to help children learn and in ways to break down the curriculum and adapt teaching methods.

In the classroom, teachers rarely get feedback about how they are doing unless they are being observed or evaluated by administrators. Co-teachers can give each other feedback on a regular basis. Each teacher should have the opportunity to sit back and observe the classroom interactions while the co-teacher directs the action of the children and carries out direct instruction.

Another benefit of co-teaching is that some teaching methods work better when there is more than one teacher in the room. Science experiments and other hands-on activities are easier to manage with two teachers. The discovery and hands-on approach is very beneficial to students with learning disabilities and attention deficit/hyperactive disorders.

Co-teaching makes classroom management easier. There are two teachers who can observe and intervene to prevent classroom disruption, if needed. If a student has an emotional outburst or is upset about something that happened at home, on the bus, or in the hall, one of the two co-teachers can give some one-to-one attention to the student while the other teacher continues to teach the rest of the class.

Co-teachers make classroom assessment more effective as well. Students can choose between written and oral versions of a test if this accommodation is necessary. And there is less loss of valuable instruction time when one of the co-teachers is absent. The remaining teacher knows the students, the routines, and the curriculum and can help a substitute teacher get acclimated to the setting.

Cooperative learning is a popular teaching method that is well served by a co-teaching model. Both teachers can move around to assist the cooperative learning groups with either process or content issues. They can also give more frequent feedback to the students than a single teacher could.

Some challenges to co-teaching do exist. First, the building administrator must recognize the importance of the model and respect the necessity of the teachers who work together to be successful. When one teacher is absent, a substitute should be obtained to preserve the model. If the administrator calls out one or more of the teachers to cover other rooms in the building, the model will suffer and the teachers may become resentful.

Administrators must respect class size if the co-teachers are willing to take on classes with ten or twelve students who have been identified for special education. If they are given the same number of students as two teachers who are not co-teaching, the purpose of co-teaching is diluted or lost.

In summary, the major benefits for those who co-teach are

- Shared responsibility for all the students in the room.
- An ongoing collaborative relationship for support.
- Encouragement for trying out new strategies—they can jointly take risks that they might not have taken as individuals.
- Appreciation for the varying kinds of expertise on the team.
- A synergy that comes from the joint effort.
- The building of strong working relationships by working together in a co-teaching situation (Pugach and Johnson, 1993).

The benefits of co-teaching are greater than the challenges. It is a practice that should be supported by teachers, administrators, and families. The model provides students with special needs the extra support they need to succeed in the general education classroom. Further, the model prevents the general education teacher from feeling like he or she has been given the students who need special assistance without receiving any assistance him- or herself.

GRADING PROCEDURES

Should a student with disabilities who receives accommodations in the classroom receive the same grade as a nondisabled peer who receives no special assistance? Teachers weigh in on both sides of this question. Some feel that if the children are already having assignments modified, this levels the playing field. Others feel that if the child needs the accommodations and can succeed in the inclusionary setting, the grading scale should also be modified if needed. As long as students with disabilities are passing their classes, do the grades really matter? Low grades are a factor in the high dropout rate for students with learning disabilities (Gersten, Vaughn, and Brengleman, 1996).

WHY DO WE GRADE STUDENTS?

The purpose of grading is to communicate student learning in relation to that of others on a nationwide, state, district, and school level to families and other interested parties. The assignment of a letter or numerical grade gives a global picture of where a student is in relation to a scale, but the student's progress toward achieving individual IEP goals and objectives is not apparent in the traditional system of grading. The school or local school district may set policy regarding grading scales.

WHO DECIDES ON THE REQUIREMENTS FOR GRADING?

The IEP should be the guiding framework for students who are receiving special education services. The general educator and the special educator should collaborate to lay out the accomplishments necessary to achieve a certain grade. It is important to keep the family informed of how grades and progress are determined.

WHAT ARE SOME CRITERIA FOR GRADING?

Bradley and Calvin (1998) recommend that the following grading criteria be used when determining the merits of the system(s) of grading that is established by a school or by individual teachers:

- Assess frequently. Long periods without communication of progress are not helpful to students, parents, or teachers.
- Analyze learning through a variety of critical elements, such as the quality of the product, the progress being made, and the process being used, such as effort and work habits.
- Give feedback to parents and students that accurately conveys achievement.
- Give feedback to students that gives them direction for improvement.

WHAT ARE SOME ALTERNATIVES FOR GRADING BEYOND LETTER GRADES AND PERCENTAGES?

Bursuck and his colleagues (1996) in a national survey of over 300 teachers (K–12) in the United States have found that teachers already use several alternative forms of grading in addition to the traditional letter grades or percentage systems in classes that are relatively homogeneous. These practices include pass/fail grades, multiple grades, grading for effort, and portfolio grading. Teachers have found these adaptations of grading to be useful for all children, not just those with disabilities (Bursuck et al., 1996). The teacher should consider effort and performance. Is the student really trying to comprehend and complete the work of the class? Is the student making good use of class time and resources but unable to complete the same quantity as other students? Does the student understand the concepts being presented in class?

The teacher could contract with the student in an inclusion setting. The teacher and the student agree on the quantity and quality of work needing to be completed before specific grades are assigned. The teachers could assign a shared grade for inclusion settings. Both general and special educators collaborate to assign grades to students with disabilities. This practice requires teachers to discuss grading philosophies beforehand and reach consensus on how to grade students.

The teacher could assign pass/fail grades. This option may be appropriate in some instances, but if it is used exclusively, the downside of this option is not letting students, parents, or potential employers know where the student is in relation to the class and the grade-level work expected.

The teacher could attach a letter to the report card explaining the student's progress. This option may work better at the elementary level when a teacher has fewer students. It may not be realistic for middle or high schools if a teacher has multiple students on IEPs. Technology could be employed, in this instance, to assist in reducing the paperwork required.

The teacher could use portfolios. They are self-reflective in nature and contain work samples across time to show an individual's growth and progress in learning. Typically, because portfolios are individualized, they provide no normative comparison with other students.

The teacher could use rubrics. They are useful for providing feedback to both parents and students. Their use allows a student to see exactly what elements will be required in an assignment to achieve a certain grade. A well-designed rubric will include criteria for both progress and process assessment.

Another option for the teacher is to use curriculum-based assessments (CBAs). The frequent and direct measurement of progress toward achievement of basic skills, such as facts, rules, and sequences, is documented in this procedure. CBAs use graphs and charts to document the attainment of knowledge. The teacher could also use mastery levels. Progress is measured on a frequent basis, though this has limited feedback for students on strengths and areas in need of improvement.

There is some evidence that students attribute a higher level of effort on their part when teachers make use of adapted grading systems in the classroom (Ring, 1997). When students begin to see their role in their own learning, and not attribute their success, or lack of it, to luck, chance, or favoritism, they begin to be active learners. Nothing breeds success like success, and the cycle of learned helplessness (Henley, Ramsey, and Algozzine, 2002) that many students with learning disabilities and other special needs display can be broken with authentic information that is relevant to their progress.

STRUCTURING
THE CLASSROOM
FOR SUCCESS

INVOLVING
OTHER STUDENTS:
AWARENESS ACTIVITIES

The following collection of activities can provide the teacher with a variety of ways to help students gain a wider perspective on what it really is like to be a special needs student in today's world. These activities can allow students to experience the feelings of their special needs classmates and reduce the level of misinformation they may have gathered. Each activity is designed to foster greater understanding of the special needs student and his or her life. These activities also promote acceptance and understanding for all students.

WHAT ARE SOME ACTIVITIES THAT CAN BE IMPLEMENTED IN THE ELEMENTARY CLASSROOM?

Activity 1: My View of Me

Supplies: Lamp, pencil, 11×14 green construction paper, scissors, old magazines, and glue. Directions:

1. Trace a silhouette of each student. This requires a large commitment of time. Assistance from an aide or parent volunteer is recommended. Students stand sideways at the front chalkboard (one student at a time) while a volunteer or teacher traces the silhouette with a pencil onto the long piece of green construction paper.

2. Each student cuts out his or her own silhouette and writes his or her name on the back.
3. Silhouettes are stored on a flat shelf until all are completed.
4. Using a collection of old magazines (carefully selected), the teacher instructs the students to cut out ten to fifteen positive phrases that they feel describe their personalities, hobbies, and interests. If possible, the teacher can share some phrases selected to describe him or her, such as "Brilliant," "Loves to read!" or "Soccer Star." It is best to request that each student show the total collection of phrases to the teacher *prior* to glue application in order to avoid inappropriate selections.
5. The teacher writes in black magic marker across the bottom of each silhouette, "My View of Me."
6. Students glue the phrases onto the silhouettes.
7. Completed silhouettes can be placed on the walls around the room (above the bulletin boards, for example). They are a topic of positive conversation for all who enter the classroom, and students will be proud to be a part of this project.

Activity 2: Disability Checklist for Safety

In order to promote awareness of the requirements for some special needs children, a list can be provided for students (working in teams) to check the classroom or school in general for safety and accessibility. For homework (as individuals) students can check one area they frequently visit, such as the drugstore, post office, or grocery store, for safety and accessibility. Wheelchair use is suggested as the best place to start. Students check safe or unsafe for wheelchair use in each of the following areas, and additional areas can be added as needed:

- Clutter on floor.
- Door wide enough for wheelchair.
- Door opens easily.
- Furniture allows for access.
- Counter space too high.
- Other items out of reach.
- Other safety hazards.

Additional areas to be added to the homework assignment might include smooth sidewalks, ramp availability, and the height of door handles. As a follow-up activity, students could create a poster about the safety hazards that were discovered. They could follow up this activity with letters to businesses requesting that the required changes be implemented.

Activity 3: Learning Stations—An Obstacle Course

Teachers may select four to six ideas from the list below or add their own ideas. They should prepare four to six learning stations and divide students into small groups of four. Students progress in numerical order through the stations until completion. Groups are numbered and begin at the same station number as their group numbers. Teachers should provide approximately fifteen minutes for each station. The activity can be extended to two days, if desired. After *each* station, students write in their journals for one minute about their feelings at that station. Then they move on to the next station and follow the same procedures. A list of the stations should be posted for easy access. Some center ideas may include the following:

1. Area: Vision
   Supplies: scarves for blindfolds and four small puzzles. Directions: Wearing blindfolds, students try to place simple puzzle pieces together.
2. Area: Writing
   Supplies: paper and pencils. Directions: The student writes his or her name and phone number with the nondominant hand and the other hand placed behind his or her back.
3. Area: Small Motor Skills
   Supplies: pencils and small boxes. Directions: Using only the last two fingers on the nondominant hand, the student picks up pencils (one at a time) and places each in a small box. Pegs can be substituted for pencils.
4. Area: Coordination
   Supplies: ruler and tape. Directions: With a ruler taped behind the knee, the student walks around the classroom stiff-legged.
5. Area: Mobility
   Supplies: wheelchair. Directions: Sitting in a wheelchair, the student tries to maneuver from one place to another in the classroom.

6. Area: Vision
   Supplies: scarves. Directions: While blindfolded, one student follows the directions provided by another student to walk around classroom obstacles. *Caution: Careful supervision is required.*

7. Area: Reading
   Supplies: mirrors and books. Directions: The student attempts to read a page in a book by looking at its reflection in the mirror.

8. Area: Physical/Fine Motor Skills
   Supplies: rubber gloves, needles, and thread. Directions: The student threads a needle while wearing two pairs of rubber gloves.

9. Area: Physical/Fine Motor Skills
   Supplies: large men's shirts and rubber gloves. Directions: The teacher asks the student to put on a shirt and button it while wearing two pairs of rubber gloves.

10. Area: Physical Disability
    Supplies: pencils. Directions: The teacher asks the students to write their names by holding *their own* pencils in their mouths with both hands behind their backs. Writing with the nondominant hand may be substituted for this activity or used as an extension. *Caution: Each should use his or her own pencil—no sharing.*

Teachers may hold a class debriefing after the final session to share student responses from these activities.

Activity 4: What Do You Do Best?

Everyone has activities that are easy to do and some that are difficult. This exercise promotes awareness of the fact that *everyone* has areas of strength and weakness. Students should check off whether the following activities are "easy" or "hard":

- Answering a question in class.
- Climbing a tree.
- Doing a long division problem.
- Drawing a picture.
- Jumping rope.

- Memorizing multiplication tables.
- Playing soccer.
- Programming the VCR.
- Rollerblading.
- Swimming.
- Using the Internet.
- Understanding fractions.
- Writing a report.

Students indicate the level of difficulty for each activity. The class can then graph the information to illustrate that everyone has difficulty with something. Items can be added to the list to create a best fit for each particular classroom.

Additional Activities

Teachers may try other activities, including the following:

- Have students read a story about Louis Braille, a French organist and teacher of the blind, who developed the Braille alphabet.
- Ask students to try to read a story or two in Braille. Braille children's books are readily available in many public libraries in the children's section. The children's librarian there can recommend these excellent resources.
- Have them try writing a story in English and in Braille.
- Invite district specialists who work with students with visual impairments to speak to the class on current issues.
- Hold an "Everybody Is Special" Activities Day and plan activities to share with other classes in the school.
- Have students create a unique alphabet and write a story using this alphabet. Invite their classmates to try to read the stories.
- Borrow a wheelchair for a week, if possible. Take turns with each student spending one hour in the wheelchair participating in all class activities.
- Using sign language, present a story to the class. After this experience, a lesson in sign language will be meaningful.
- Invite an outside speaker or guest to read a story in another language to the class. Follow this with a discussion on how the activity impacted the students.

- Ask students to write autobiographies or complete fill-in-the-blank worksheets about themselves.
- Pair a special needs student with a general education student and assign each the task of interviewing the other. Then each interviewee should present the information on the partner to the class. Specific questions should be provided by the teacher.
- Play a bingo-like game called "Who's Who in Room 217?" Create a bingo card with a series of up to twenty-five statements, for example, "Someone who is wearing glasses." Provide a copy of the sheet to each student. Students are given a specific allotment of time and are to request a student's signature that fits the description. Each student may sign another student's card *only* one time.
- Ask students to create poems about themselves using haiku, cinquain, or other poetry forms.
- Invite guest speakers who have special needs themselves to share about their lives.
- Create a class list called "Famous People with Special Needs." Ask each student to select the person of his or her choice and write/present a report on that person.
- Read aloud stories about special needs children.
- Create a scrapbook of news and magazine articles about people with special needs who make the news.
- Create a "Star of the Week" bulletin board. The teacher can volunteer to be first. In order to be the "Star of the Week" each student should write one paragraph about him- or herself. In addition, pictures of oneself, pets, vacations, family members, favorite books, and hobbies may be added to complete a colorful bulletin board. All items should be submitted to the teacher one week prior to being posted. Students could sign up for a specific week or partial week, depending on the number of students in the class. Every student should have an opportunity to be the star.

These activities create a high level of interest among classmates, teachers, and families. They heighten both awareness and understanding of the students with special needs in the classroom. These activities have been successfully implemented in elementary classrooms.

PARENTS AS PARTNERS

Parents play a key role in the education of the student in the inclusive classroom. During the past century, parents have been powerful advocates in the initiation of inclusive services for children with special needs. Many professionals believe that family participation is a critical factor in the success of all students in inclusive classrooms. Regular communication between the teacher and the parent(s) provides useful information and promotes an ongoing relationship that is beneficial to all.

WHAT ARE THE BARRIERS THAT KEEP PARENTS FROM PARTICIPATING IN SCHOOL?

Educators often see lack of parent involvement as apathy. Frequently, it is just the opposite. Teachers need to recognize that a parent's own past school experiences can affect the comfort level for current classroom involvement. In order to encourage a high level of parent involvement, educators should make volunteering in the classroom a parent-friendly endeavor.

Time constraints are primary stumbling blocks for parents whose work schedules are inflexible. If both parents work and will lose pay by taking time off to come to school, there is little incentive for involvement. Young mothers with large families are also prohibited from coming because of lack of opportunities for child care. It is important for the message from the school to meet the needs of the varieties of parent/family situations. Then, and only then, will the level of parent involvement rise, with parents feeling that the school is a caring place.

HOW CAN SCHOOLS BETTER ENCOURAGE PARENTAL INVOLVEMENT?

The following strategies are geared to improve the relationships between parents and teachers in inclusive classrooms while at the same time encouraging parent participation in school:

- Meet with the parents prior to student placement in the inclusive classroom. This provides the teacher with the opportunity to make positive contact before the school year begins.
- Contact students early. Students like to get mail, and a postcard notifying them of assignment to a teacher's class (positively stated) will be enthusiastically welcomed. Parents will take note of this.
- Focus on encouraging parent involvement. Find out the reasons why parents may be reluctant to get involved (minimal schooling, feelings of inferiority, time constraints on the job, personal limitations, linguistic and cultural differences) and be determined to remove these obstacles.
- Clarify detailed ways in which parents can help. Minor things, such as sending home a list requesting empty jar lids for an art project, can encourage initial involvement on the part of reluctant parents. Once praised for this response, parents become more willing to try again.
- Develop trust. The best way to develop trust is the way in which the teacher treats the children in the class. Nothing creates trust faster than positive responses coming out of the mouths of children.
- Invite parents to drama or project presentations. Create small, simple presentations to encourage parent involvement. Keep presentations short and extend invitations, which include small siblings or provide child care service. Every parent likes to see his or her child perform.
- Help establish parent support groups. The school guidance counselor may be willing to assist in the development of these groups. This takes time and patience but is worth the wait if teachers have other parents who share the desire to be involved in their children's school experience.

- Involve the students in encouraging parental involvement. As the teacher, one can be an enabler when providing nonthreatening opportunities for parental involvement.
- Develop homework assignments that encourage total family involvement. Include bilingual activities whenever possible.
- Build on home experiences. Invite children to share cultural holidays or special family occasions.
- Use parental expertise. Telephone conversations or questionnaires can lead to information regarding hobbies or interests that can be shared in the classroom or in a small group.
- Send positive notes home frequently. Everyone, child and adult alike, responds positively to a compliment.
- Keep parents aware of timelines for projects, field trips, and activities at school.

WHAT ARE THE MOST SUCCESSFUL WAYS TO COMMUNICATE WITH PARENTS?

Communication is a critical element in any collaboration between the teacher and the parent. Parents often complain that there is too little communication between the home and the school. Problems that arise could often be avoided if there were meaningful communication. Research shows that a major effort is needed to improve communication between parents and teachers (Smith et al., 1995). Parents should never feel that they are being "talked down to" but, rather, that they are partners with the teacher in the educational process of the child. The following are important communication tools:

- Informal Notes: Written notes to parents can be an effective way to communicate progress, send a compliment, or include information. The teacher should keep the note simple so that it is readily understandable. It is best to include a way for the parents to respond to the note.
- Phone Calls: This is an efficient means of communication with most parents. It is important to make the initial calls (and as many as possible thereafter) positive calls. The first call may simply be to state that a teacher is pleased to have the student in his or her class. Be certain to

provide the parent with a phone number where the teacher may be reached.

- Parent Visits: Whenever possible, parents should be invited to make informal classroom visits. Occasions such as drama presentations, choral renditions, debates, and poster sessions are readily shared with parents in the audience. Informal occasions such as these provide the parents with the opportunity to see their children's class and teacher at work and to promote positive feelings about life at school.

- Newsletters: These items should be brief, frequent, and eye-catching. If possible, the teacher could include examples of student work from time to time in the newsletter. It is best to keep newsletters simple and positive.

WHAT ABOUT PARENT-TEACHER CONFERENCES?

It is vital that parents feel welcome to participate in parent conferences. In order to maximize family involvement, teachers may need to become more proactive in soliciting parental participation. Simply issuing an invitation to attend is not enough. A few items to consider are the following:

- Clarify the purpose of the conference.
- Prepare a list of concerns and strengths.
- Hold the conference in a place with few, if any, distractions.
- Maintain a timely schedule and do not run overtime.
- Arrange the room so that teacher and parent can face each other without barriers.
- Provide the parent with an opportunity to speak first, if he or she so wishes.
- Present the *child's* strengths first.
- Be sure to do as much listening as talking.
- Avoid the use of acronyms and educational jargon.
- Let the parent know that the teacher is available in the future when needed.
- Always conclude on a positive note.

- Prepare a brief, dated conference summary for the record. This should include any extensions of the conference that are needed.

Remember, communication with parents should convey the important message that they are needed and valued as important members of the educational team committed to their children's educational progress. Quality communication should be a high priority.

INTERDISCIPLINARY
AND INTEGRATED
CURRICULUM

There is a trend in education toward a more integrated curriculum (Sadker and Sadker, 1997). An integrated curriculum pulls from the common themes or concepts across subjects. It is a model of curriculum that does not compartmentalize subjects as if they were discrete bodies of knowledge. Real life is not compartmentalized. Adults usually need to draw on their knowledge of several fields to solve problems (Glatthorn, 1994).

Integration should be a consideration in curriculum design. It involves linking all types of knowledge and experiences "to bring into close relationship all the bits and pieces of the curriculum in ways that enable the individual to comprehend knowledge as unified, rather than as atomized" (Ornstein and Hunkins, 1998, p. 240). Making connections across and between disciplines increases the likelihood of understanding, retention, and application (Palmer, 1995). Many terms have been used in curriculum studies to get at the same idea: *connected curriculum, integrated curriculum, interdisciplinary curriculum,* and *curricular connections.* It can be confusing to hear curriculum experts using new jargon for the same idea.

Curriculum integration makes sense because of the tremendous growth in knowledge that has occurred, the need to reduce the fragmentation of the school day, and the need to develop a relevant curriculum to retain students in school (Jacobs, 1989). Methodology and language from more than one discipline are used "to examine a central theme, issue, problem, topic or experience" (Jacobs, 1989, p. 8). It is the linkages that are stressed in the process.

Students with special needs may have an easier time learning the content of a course when teachers use an interdisciplinary curriculum. Not all students learn in the same way. Teachers must strive to find ways to reach each and every student. Students with learning disabilities, in particular, often do not see connections among their school subjects. The provision of an interdisciplinary curriculum does not ensure that all students will master the content. Teachers make choices about the essential subject area knowledge of their discipline. A method for making these decisions is called "differentiated instruction" (Tomlinson, 1999a). The principles of a differentiated classroom are as follows:

- the teacher focuses on the essentials;
- the teacher attends to student differences;
- assessment and instruction are inseparable;
- the teacher modifies content, process, and products;
- all students participate in respectful work;
- the teacher and students collaborate in learning;
- the teacher balances group and individual norms; and
- the teacher and students work together flexibly.

Differentiated learning is an organized, yet flexible, way of providing instruction in the curriculum that meets the needs of all learners. Learning needs to be "whole," important, and meaning making (Tomlinson, 1999b). Teachers are being encouraged to "differentiate" their instruction. By paying attention to the "how" of teaching, educators can meet the differing needs of their students across ability levels. Teachers need to know where they are going if they hope to lead their students on the journey. Knowing where they are going with a subject, class, or lesson takes a plan (Tomlinson, 1999a). It is in the "how" of learning that teachers are able to vary their techniques by using a variety of working arrangements, allowing for different modes of expression, and using various forms of scaffolding. Differentiation of instruction works best when teachers know their intended outcomes: "If the 'stuff' is ill conceived, the 'how' is doomed" (Tomlinson, 1999a, p. 16).

By using differentiated instruction the teacher is able to respond to the needs of all learners in the classroom. Each individual student's needs are considered in this framework. Separate accommodations for students with special needs may not be necessary.

Teachers should take a careful look at a lesson plan that has been developed and ask key questions:

- What is expected of students in this lesson?
- Will students with disabilities be able to achieve the goals of the lesson? If the answer is yes, then no further accommodations to the plan are needed. If the answer is no, then the teacher needs to ask, What *can* the students with disabilities do?
- Will it help if different materials are provided?
- Will students be able to do parts of the lesson as it is presented?
- Will it help to present the lesson in a different way?
- Will it work if students are grouped for the activity rather than having each individual student complete the assignment independently?

As teams of teachers plan for an integrated curriculum, these teaching considerations should be kept in mind:

- What is the objective?
- What should students learn from this lesson?
- Will all of the students in the classroom be able to do the lesson as written?

Elementary teachers, by the very nature of their work, are more likely to integrate curriculum than secondary teachers. Most elementary teachers have the same group of students for a long block of time on a daily basis. Contrast this with a forty-five-, fifty-five-, or ninety-minute block of time at the secondary level. The content preparation of most elementary teachers is broader and more interdisciplinary than that of secondary teachers who major in a specific discipline. Secondary teachers have the depth of subject matter but not the breadth that may be needed for interdisciplinary curriculum development.

When teachers decide to integrate curriculum they have options for how to begin (Glatthorn, 1994; Jacobs, 1989). Glatthorn presents two basic ways: (a) integration while keeping subjects separate and (b) integration of two or more subjects. Integration while keeping subjects separate may be accomplished by

- Correlating two subjects—for example, teaching colonial history and colonial literature together.
- Integrating skills *across* disciplines—for example, reading, writing, thinking, and learning.
- Integrating skills *within* disciplines—for example, whole language or unified science.
- Informally integrating—for example, bringing in one content area while teaching another.

Integration of *two or more* subjects may be

- Subject focused—for example, "colonial history" as examined by reading primary source materials in colonial journals and documents.
- Theme focused—for example, "hurricanes" as examined by reading scientific explanations in texts and on the Internet, reading fiction and nonfiction accounts of hurricanes, viewing films about the theme, noting mathematical calculations of wind speed, using geographical study by tracking the coordinates of approaching hurricanes, and so on.
- Project focused—for example, a "Stop Smoking Campaign" designed around student research into the effects of smoking on the body and secondhand smoke, survey research with medical professionals, graphing data from interviews and surveys, and creation of an advertising campaign for the National Smoke Out Day.
- Focused in any other creative ways teachers may develop.

Another model of integrating instruction is Integrated Thematic Instruction (ITI). Kovalik (1994) and Ross and Olsen (1995) have linked their integrated thematic teaching to brain research. This research reveals that the brain has a tremendous capacity to reorganize information around prior knowledge. Learning can occur for all students, at all levels of development, and at all ages. Kovalik recommends that elementary teachers start organizing around science as a content area of study. Science is "the understanding of how the natural world works and the implications of man's interactions with it" (Kovalik, 1994, p. 1). Next, organize around social studies, which is "the story of the needs and expectations of groups, communities, and societies" (Kovalik, 1994, p. 1).

The tenets behind ITI are

- The absence of threat (focus on life skills).
- Meaningful content (focus on real life).
- Choices (focus on multiple intelligences).
- Adequate time.
- Enriched environment.
- Collaboration.
- Immediate feedback.
- Mastery.

Sufficient planning time, staff development, and a flexible curriculum provide teachers with optimal conditions for beginning to use an interdisciplinary curriculum in their classrooms (Palmer, 1995). Teachers need to use a model as a structure. Palmer (1995) describes a simple device called a Planning Wheel that has been used in some school districts. The wheel has the main focus of the content at its hub. The various content area activities are on the rim of the wheel. Spokes leading out to the rim from the center contain the objective, thinking skills, and assessment design planned for each activity. The wheel provides teachers with a visual depiction of the big ideas of their integrated units.

There are some barriers to interdisciplinary teaching. Concerns about interdisciplinary teaching have to do with the fear that one discipline will dominate another. There are also worries that important content may be lost and students may not obtain the depth of the subject they need to pass mandated standardized tests. There is worry that a subject, such as math, will be taught only in relation to another, such as science, and that it will lose its status as a separate subject. Staff development personnel can help teachers face these barriers. In a well-designed integrated unit, less content can often result in more learning: "less is more." By focusing on having clear objectives and well-defined performance expectations, an interdisciplinary curriculum can succeed and meet the needs of all learners in an inclusion classroom, provided the students are properly placed with the supports they need.

STRATEGIES
FOR SUCCESS

**ARE THERE SPECIFIC THINGS TO CONSIDER WHEN
IMPLEMENTING WHOLE GROUP INSTRUCTION IN THE
INCLUSIVE CLASSROOM?**

In the inclusive classroom, as in any classroom, the first consideration for the teacher is to express high expectations for success for each and every student. Teachers teach to their strengths, so most teachers will implement strategies they like and with which they feel comfortable. In addition, the teacher should stretch his or her thinking to constantly evaluate new ideas and strategies to ensure success for all students. Tasks selected should be meaningful, related to real life, and provide multiple paths to solutions rather than just one. The teacher in the inclusive classroom should be aware of the learning styles and multiple intelligences of each student. The implementation of new strategies should be shared with families, if at all possible.

**WHAT ABOUT USING COOPERATIVE GROUPING
IN THE INCLUSIVE CLASSROOM?**

Cooperative learning is firmly advocated for the inclusive classroom. Students who might be hesitant to speak before the class as a whole seem to feel comfortable expressing opinions in a small group of four members. It is vital that the procedures for cooperative learning, along with the rules and results, are clearly explained and modeled prior to implementation. It is imperative that quality tasks be selected and tried by the teacher prior to implementation with the class.

ARE THERE SPECIFIC TEACHING STRATEGIES THAT CAN BE USED IN AN INCLUSIVE CLASSROOM?

There are numerous strategies that lead to success in both the general education classroom and the inclusive classroom. Some successful strategies follow:

1. Learning Centers: Teachers have used learning centers for many years. The learning center is an area in the classroom that houses a collection of materials to teach or extend a concept. Centers are unique in that each one stands alone. Teachers may create a math center, science center, art center, writing center, and more. Students usually rotate through centers. Different teachers use and define centers in a variety of ways.

2. Interest Centers: An interest center is created to appeal to a particular area of interest to a student or students. All centers should focus on class learning goals, use activities that address a wide variety of learning styles and interests, vary from simple to complex, provide clear succinct directions, and include a record-keeping system.

3. Learning Contracts: Learning contracts have been used for many years in elementary school classrooms. A contract is a negotiated agreement between the student and the teacher and often allows some student choice. In the learning contract, the teacher specifically states what is expected (in detail) and the time frame in which the task is to be accomplished. The contract usually contains notation of positive consequences when the contract is fulfilled. Each contract should include the signature of the student and the teacher along with the date on which it is signed. Some contracts allow for checkpoints along the way in order to keep the student on task.

4. Graphic Organizers: Story maps, story webs, and outlines of any form help the learner to organize his or her thinking. Organizing the material in advance of the written assignment helps students categorize their thinking in a logical manner. This type of activity is most successful when first modeled by the teacher with the whole class on a regular basis. After several weeks, students can be expected to implement the use of this strategy on their own.

5. Problem-Based Learning: This particular learning tactic places students in a problem-solving situation similar to a real job situation. The teacher provides the group of students with a vague but complex problem to solve. Students must seek outside information, define the problem carefully, locate valid resources, propose a solution, and present it to their classmates.

6. Group Interest Investigation: For group investigations, students select a book, activity, or project based solely on their common interests. After students divide into interest groups, the teacher can provide guidelines for the progress of the investigation and the expected end product.

7. Positive Reinforcement: This strategy has a successful history. The teacher catches the student doing something good and praises the student to the entire class. The compliment is a strong reinforcement of approved behavior.

8. Mnemonics: When students must memorize information in a specific order such as the order of the planets or the keys on the piano, a sentence is created beginning with the first letter of each planet or key. Using rhyme or songs to assist with memorization is also an efficient technique. These strategies are beneficial for all students but are especially effective in inclusive classrooms.

9. Cue Cards: Some students may benefit from the use of cue cards on their desks or a cue poster in the front of the room. Vocabulary and spelling terms should be in full sight and available to decrease stumbling blocks and ensure student success in the activity.

10. Task Analysis: Task analysis involves the breaking down of a large assignment into small, workable tasks. In so doing, the student feels successful in checking off each small incremental task, rather than being bogged down by the entire assignment.

11. Peer Tutoring: Students often learn best from other students. Students from the same or a neighboring classroom may act as tutors for their peers. Another exciting way to adapt peer tutoring is to involve special needs students in a tutoring program with very young students (kindergarten) to assist in the learning of the alphabet sounds or number facts.

12. Choice Boards: When using choice boards, assignments are placed in different pockets. Each particular row of assignments targets one skill or need. Teachers ask students to select or choose an activity from one par-

ticular row, thereby providing each student with a choice in the needed assignment or required skill.

13. Technology: The use of technology in the schools is transforming schooling while encouraging excitement for learning in all children. Technology refers to computers, but it also includes calculators, VCRs, video cameras, scanners, CDs, and laser videodisks. Multiple uses of technology have assisted students with disabilities to access the needed curriculum and communicate their knowledge. Technology is seen as a tool that helps remove barriers to learning and promotes success.

CLASSROOM
IMPLEMENTATION

SOCIAL SKILL
DEVELOPMENT

What is the connection between how a student learns and the student's self-concept? How can a teacher foster positive relationships in the classroom? When a student does not feel good about the way he or she looks or the way he or she is perceived in the classroom, learning can suffer. Rather than being focused on learning, the student may spend valuable time on negative thoughts. Teachers need to find ways to enhance self-concept on a daily basis for all students, particularly for those students with special needs. How do teachers accomplish this? Teachers can

- Make it a point to learn each student's interests, talents, and preferences.
- Give students who have academic difficulties a chance to succeed in other areas, such as art, music, or sports.
- Have high expectations for all students in the class, including those with learning difficulties.
- Remember how important their influence is in the building of self-esteem—teachers have more influence than they realize over this aspect of student development.
- Address the student's learning difficulties in a straightforward way—many students, particularly those with mild disabilities, do not understand why they are receiving special education services.

Teachers understand that students with disabilities may have academic difficulties. Students may struggle with some of the subject matter, and, if so, accommodations should be made. However, teachers may not be prepared to meet
the social and emotional needs of these students. Social skill development is an
area of concern for teachers of students with learning and behavior problems.
Obtaining and holding a job may be based more on a person's social skills than
on his or her technical or professional skills. Research has found students with
learning disabilities and behavior disorders to have some of the following types
of problems that directly relate to social skills:

- Difficulty expressing feelings.
- Difficulty in feeling empathy for others.
- An inability to take the perspective of another.
- A lack of self-confidence and a tendency to portray learned helplessness
  behaviors.
- Less proficiency in planning for the future.
- More likelihood to approach a teacher with inappropriate questions
  (Vaughn, Bos, and Schumm, 2000).

Any one of the problems listed above can cause difficulty for a student in the
classroom, and many teachers feel unprepared to teach students about social
skills. There are a number of commercial programs that have been designed for
teachers to use in the area of social skill development. Educators are searching
for ways to teach character development because school violence has become a
strong concern in U.S. schools. With increased pressure for higher academic
standards, most teachers simply do not feel that they have the time to add instruction in social skills to their curriculum.

Many of the necessary social skills needed by students with exceptionalities
could be woven into a curriculum that is already being taught in the classroom.
This integration would keep teachers from feeling burdened by another curriculum responsibility. Students who need help with social skills are provided
for in the mainstream of classroom activities. It is not necessary to have a separate, pullout activity for a group of students. Problem-solving and role-playing
activities are built into many character education programs.

Vaughn and La Greca (1993) have outlined three principles that should be
considered when a teacher is doing social skills instruction:

1. Provide effective instruction, such as getting the students' commitment to learn the skills, pretest, describe the strategy, identify the steps of the strategy, allow students to role-play, and teach them to self-monitor their use of the strategy.
2. Involve peers in the instruction; it is not just for the students who have social skills development in their IEPs. By doing this, the teacher lets all the students know what is being worked on, not just the target student. The others are more likely to accept changes and to reinforce the changes if they know the goals of the instruction.
3. Teach for transfer of learning and generalization. Teachers can do this by varying the setting, the teacher, the materials, the task, and the cues given to the students. This helps prevent the documented phenomenon of a student learning a skill in one setting but failing to use it in other appropriate settings.

The direct teaching of social skills is important because it provides the students with appropriate social behavior that may be used in situations that previously provoked a negative response. In a typical situation in which a student displays a behavior that is perceived as rude by other students, the student would be directed to stop the behavior. The teacher might then look for a positive behavior that can be praised in an attempt to shape a new behavior. Behaviors are strengthened when they are reinforced. Unfortunately, this works for negative as well as positive reinforcement. With an approach such as "skillstreaming" (McGinnis and Goldstein, 1997), students are taught pro-social behaviors in role-play situations. The program is very systematic. It is designed to enhance self-esteem, provide encouragement, help prevent violence, and remediate students who are severely lacking in social skills.

The basis for the direct teaching of social skills is social learning theory. Albert Bandura (1973) is particularly well known for his work in this area. His research has found that modeling, practicing the behaviors, and social reinforcement are crucial to the learning of new behaviors. The behavioral approach has been successful in increasing the positive behavior of a student if the behavior is already part of the student's repertoire. Many of the students in our schools today do not have a strong bank of behaviors that teachers can reinforce; therefore, programs such as skillstreaming are being used by educators to fill the void.

Teachers use these programs to directly teach pro-social skills. For example, the elementary-level curriculum for skillstreaming (McGinnis and Goldstein, 1997) has five strands. These are

- Classroom survival (thirteen skills).
- Friendship making (twelve skills).
- Dealing with feelings (ten skills).
- Alternatives to aggression (nine skills).
- Dealing with stress (sixteen skills).

Combining the school reform initiatives and the safe schools initiatives has put more of a focus on schoolwide climate, reduction of school violence, schoolwide discipline plans, and, in general, a coordinated curriculum that promotes such an environment. School culture strongly determines the curriculum of a school. Students are participating in schoolwide mediation programs on an increasing basis. They are also being included in setting school rules and taking the responsibility for following them. Delving into recent school violence incidents in the United States has uncovered portraits of students who are alienated from their school culture. Students and parents want their schools to be safe and welcoming places without feelings of isolation and alienation.

Social skills are relevant for today's schools and today's students. It is natural to include the teaching of them as part of a well-rounded curriculum. The choice of how to include social skills development ultimately rests within the school. Teachers may use a standard published social skills curriculum, include social skills as part of character education, or infuse the social skills into their everyday curriculum. The inclusion of social skills instruction is an important aspect of curriculum for today's educators.

COMMUNICATION AND COLLABORATION

WHY IS COLLABORATION IMPORTANT?

Teachers can do more working together than working alone to solve problems. Any new or challenging situation can be faced more confidently when a teacher is part of a team trying to develop the best possible program for a student. Collaboration is even more crucial when the student has special needs.

Teachers without certification in special education often feel unprepared to meet the needs of students requiring special education services in the general education classroom. On the other hand, the special education teacher or specialist may never have taught general education students and may have limited experience with large groups of students. By combining both sets of expertise, teachers can develop a program that is most likely to succeed for students who have special education needs.

WHAT IS COLLABORATION?

Collaboration has been defined as an "interactive process that enables groups of people with diverse expertise to generate creative solutions to mutually defined problems" (Idol, Paolucci-Whitcomb, and Nevin, 1994, p. 13). When teams of teachers decide on the real needs of the students, the synergy of the team transcends the work of any individual teacher in most instances. Teachers have four participation options for schoolwide collaboration (Turnbull et al., 2002). These options are supporter, facilitator, information giver, and prescriber. In the support role, the teacher listens to and validates the other person as he or she struggles with issues related to the inclusion of students with exceptionalities. This collaborator is there to celebrate successes and to acknowledge challenges. In the role of facilitator, the teacher helps colleagues develop the ability to solve problems and deal independently with professional challenges. The information giver provides colleagues with direct information to deal with problems. Suggestions may be based on one's own experience. In the prescriptive role, the teacher may suggest a plan of action to a colleague. In successful collaborative situations, the participants spend time in each of the four roles over the course of a school year. The roles are reciprocal; sometimes one of the collaborators is the giver, and at other times, the receiver. Collaboration is a two-way street.

WHY ARE TEACHERS BEING ASKED TO COLLABORATE?

As school populations have become more diverse across America, so too has the range of challenges to a teacher's repertoire. Problem-solving teams made up of professionals representing varied perspectives, parents with their unique viewpoint about their children, and outside-school agency representatives can collaborate to come up with creative solutions to problems. One of the results of increased collaboration has been a reduction in the number of referrals to special education as well as the return of students who have been labeled as special education students to a restructured general education classroom (Turnbull et al., 2002). Knowing that every problem situation does not have to be resolved alone gives new life to teachers who are in stressful situations.

WHERE WILL TEACHERS FIND THE TIME
TO COLLABORATE?

For collaboration to achieve its fullest potential, professionals must be given the time to do this important work. The time to do collaboration should be regarded as essential to the teacher's role, not as an adjunct or as "released time" (Raywid,

1993). School boards and the public must begin to value, and allow for, teacher work that is not counted only in terms of direct student contact hours. Planning, curriculum development, collaboration, and building team meetings for problem solving are all essential parts of an effective teacher's role. Professionals in other fields such as law get paid for all the hours spent on research and preparation for work with clients. Medical doctors, home decorators, and landscape architects, to name a few, are compensated for preparation time, not just for time spent directly with clients.

The following guidelines have been found to be valuable for productive use of time for collaboration (Raywid, 1993). Collaboration time should

- Not be scheduled at the end of the regular school day.
- Not be scheduled during the "prime time" school day.
- Not take place on weekends or holidays, even if it is compensated.

If collaboration should not take place after school or during prime school time, when can it occur? In some districts, students are sent home early one day a week for staff professional development. This time may provide an opportunity for collaboration. Another possibility is to have a common planning period combined with a shared lunchtime that is uninterrupted by duty requirements. Unless a large uninterrupted chunk of time can be found, teacher collaboration efforts will suffer.

Collaboration in schools today goes far beyond professionals discussing students with disabilities. The increase in site-based management, increased diversity in our school population, and the changing, more complex nature of instruction in today's schools are all compelling reasons for collaboration (Pugach and Johnson, 1993). The days when a teacher only had to excel with students in the classroom are long past. Teachers need a strong learning community from which to draw strength to do the complex work that awaits them in the diverse classrooms of today. Collaboration must be planned. It will not happen on its own.

IS COLLABORATION JUST FOR THE PROFESSIONAL STAFF?

Collaborative skills are an integral part of many teaching practices currently being used in schools across the country. Students are working together, or collaborating, when they are engaged in cooperative learning, cross-age learning, or peer tutoring.

At the teacher level, peer coaching of staff, collaborative planning, co-teaching, and team teaching are going on. All of these techniques require collaboration and communication among teachers. Shared decision making and site-based management allow teachers to collaborate about the operation of the school at the building level.

Is there a collaboration model for teachers? Collaboration is more likely to be successful if there is schoolwide training in an effective collaboration process. Several models of consultation between general and special education have been designed. The models provide supporting materials such as worksheets to use while working through the collaboration process (Fuchs, Fuchs, and Bahr, 1990; Pugach and Johnson, 1993; West, Idol, and Cannon, 1989). Most of the models offer a problem-solving sequence similar to the following:

- Problem identification.
- Problem analysis.
- Plan implementation.
- Problem evaluation (Fuchs, Fuchs, and Bahr, 1990).

WHAT ISSUES COMMONLY ARISE IN CONSULTATION/COLLABORATION?

When general and special educators collaborate, there are specific issues and dilemmas that commonly arise (Bos and Vaughn, 1998). Some of the typical concerns are as follows:

- Student Ownership: Yours, Mine, or Ours?: "Ours" is the most productive approach to take. It does not help the student to be referred to as "your" student by the general education teacher speaking to the special education teacher or vice versa. When both teachers collaborate to provide the best learning environment for a student, good things can happen. If there is a problem, both teachers have strength areas to bring to the collaborative session.
- Content Coverage or Student Accommodation: In the current environment of higher standards, teachers are faced with the dilemma of how to meet the diverse needs of students in their classrooms and the pressure to

"cover" the curriculum. Many teachers have responded to the issue by adopting a "less is more" philosophy to curriculum coverage (Bos and Vaughn, 1998, p. 477).

- Whole Class or Individual Student View: Researchers have found that general education teachers consider the whole class when they plan. Special education teachers look at each individual student and at how that student is learning.
- Real-World Viewpoint: Many teachers feel that accommodations will not be made for people in the real world. Therefore, students should not have accommodations in school in order to prepare them for real life. Special educators can help by pointing out that in the workplace employers are required to make needed accommodations. Teachers should only be asked to make accommodations that are beneficial to the majority of the other students in the class, as well as for the student with special needs.

CURRICULUM-CENTERED COLLABORATION

Warger and Pugach (1996) suggest that another productive way of looking at collaboration is to shift the focus of the collaboration away from the problem of the student to that of the curriculum. They call this the curriculum-centered approach. The model starts with

1. Orientation: rapport is established, it is recognized that both parties have the expertise to contribute, and the limits for collaboration are set.
2. Problem identification: identify new strategies and assessment techniques; identify new relationships among student, curriculum, teachers, and peers; identify potential mismatches; and present relevant data.
3. Intervention: come up with several ideas for instruction, assessment, and curriculum; select some strategies; identify any support needed for students and teachers; and develop a plan to implement.
4. Closure: review progress, evaluate how the lesson went, and evaluate what the students learned.

Every teacher knows that, despite the best planning and collaborating, not all lessons always go as planned. When this happens there is a tendency to blame the students: "They were not listening," "Several students with special needs did not follow directions," and so forth. When the collaboration is centered on the curriculum, the focus shifts from blame to what the teachers want the students to know and be able to do.

If the teachers involved have a clear understanding about the curriculum that is to be taught and the skills students need to succeed, the collaborative efforts will be smoother and the focus will be less on the student(s) with special needs. It becomes an issue of adapting the curriculum rather than trying to figure out how to "fix" a student who has special needs. After all, it is in knowing what teachers want their students to understand and be able to perform that true communication and collaboration around the needs of every learner in the inclusive classroom can take place.

IMPLEMENTING
TECHNOLOGY

WHY IS TECHNOLOGY APPROPRIATE FOR ALL STUDENTS?

The pace of change occurring in the computer technology field is extremely rapid. New technologies seem to enter the market on a daily basis. Many of these new technologies are useful in improving the lives of students with special needs. Research illustrates that the use of computer technology is beneficial for these students and for all students. Some of the current and future uses of computers in the inclusive classroom are as follows:

1. Word Processing: Word processing serves as a beneficial tool for special needs and general education students, especially those who have difficulties with spelling, handwriting, and written documents or projects. Many teachers feel that learning word-processing skills should be mandatory for all students, not just those with special needs.
2. World Wide Web and E-mail: Using a computer, a modem, a telephone line, and access to an online service, students can enter the "information highway" of today. Students can access information for reports and send/receive e-mail around the globe. They can link onto sites of particular information for their areas of interest and do so at any time of the day or night.
3. CD-ROM Technology: Many classroom computer systems now contain CD-ROM drives. Compact discs contain multimedia applications, with

each disc containing a large storage and retrieval capacity. Students using this technology can access encyclopedia information.

4. Assistive Technology: This type of technology refers to devices that enable special needs students to participate actively in numerous activities that would otherwise be unavailable to them without the use of a computer. The Technology Act, which was first passed by Congress in 1988 and was reauthorized in 1994, recognizes the need for special needs students to use assistive technology devices. The act also provides funding to support assistive technology. Three specific ways in which students can use assistive technology to overcome barriers follow (Lewis, 1998):

   • *Overcoming Print Barriers:* There are varied assistive devices to help students who have problems with reading and writing skills. Options include talking computer programs, taped books, and devices that read books aloud.

   • *Overcoming Learning Barriers:* Audiotapes, CD-ROM instruction, use of the Internet, and videodisc instruction can be of assistance in learning for all students.

   • *Overcoming Communication Barriers:* For assistance in the area of written communication, programs include word processing, spelling and grammar checks, organizational programs, and voice input that allows the student to record a written message.

   Numerous writers have demonstrated the effectiveness of using assistive technology to enhance the learning of all students. Special needs students may require a variety of adaptations to ensure their success in school. Assistive technology devices may serve as possible solutions to help students achieve maximum success in the classroom. Devices such as word processors, reading machines, talking computers, speech recognition systems, electronic spell checkers, and educational software appear to foster independence and promote academic success for students with learning disabilities and to help other students compensate for academic difficulties (Bryant and Seay, 1998).

5. Videodiscs: Videodiscs are another useful tool for the inclusive classroom. Containing information just like a videotape, a videodisc can randomly access information and can store thousands of frames of graphics, text, and slides. Interactive videodiscs allow students to see real-life simulations on the monitor in their classroom.

6. Instructional Software: There are virtually thousands of software programs available for every age and curriculum level. Finding and evaluating
   the best software for the classroom is an awesome task. Education and professional journals often evaluate, review, and recommend software for varied purposes and age/grade levels. These reviews can be used as an initial
   screening device for classroom software needs. Software should always be
   previewed prior to classroom use. Only the teacher can decide whether
   the quality of information is appropriate for the class of students in that
   setting. Consultation with other teachers and with the media specialist is
   recommended. Software should appear flexible, be easy to use, be age appropriate, contain quality content, allow for easy feedback, contain clear
   directions, and present a pleasing screen design.

7. Spreadsheets: Spreadsheets can assist students with their mathematics in
   much the same way that word-processing programs help with their writing. Spreadsheets organize numerical information into rows and columns
   and are beneficial to use when calculating and analyzing numerical data.

WHAT TECHNOLOGY ADAPTATIONS ARE APPROPRIATE FOR INCLUSIVE CLASSROOMS?

It is most important that each individual be evaluated so that the appropriate
technology assistance can be prescribed. Technology that may be prescribed for
one student may not fit the needs of another. The student needs, the specific
task, and the academic setting must be taken into consideration. According to
the IDEA amendments of 1997, the IEP team should consider whether a child
needs assistive technology devices to ensure academic success. Bryant, Bryant,
and Raskind (1998) have presented a process that can be used to evaluate students and their learning environments to identify the best assistive technology
for students. Bryant and Bryant (1998) provide some sample questions to be
considered for the evaluation of assistive technology needs. They are as follows:

- What are the tasks to be performed?
- What are the student's strengths and weaknesses?
- What are the student's needs, and how do they impact the ability to com-
  plete the assigned tasks?

CHAPTER 19

- Are there compatibility issues with other classroom technology?
- Can the technology be used across the curriculum with varied tasks?
- Is it efficient and easy to use?
- What training is required for the student, teacher, and family?
- What environmental features should be considered (space, electrical outlets, etc.)?
- How reliable is the technology?
- To what extent does the technology promote independence?
- To what extent does the technology compensate for the disability?
- What are the opinions of the student, family, and teacher about the technology?

WHAT ARE THE ADVANTAGES OF IMPLEMENTING TECHNOLOGY IN THE INCLUSIVE CLASSROOM?

Olson and Platt (1996) state that this implementation leads to improved achievement, increased learning time, improved self-esteem, and enhanced positive attitudes toward learning. Computers in the classroom can be used to combine strategies and tailor individualized learning experiences for each student or group of students.

In summary, the computer has been found to be a useful tool to enhance students' capabilities and to increase the quality and efficiency of their work. Technology is a strong support to instruction and can potentially lead to an increase in motivation, independence, and self-confidence. Technology appears to be one of the most promising ways to help all students reach their potential and achieve success. Living and teaching in a high-tech society is exciting. With student enthusiasm high regarding the implementation of technology, it is obvious that computer use can make learning more interesting, more relevant, and more exciting. In addition, it will always take an excellent teacher to plan, implement, and manage a technology program to benefit the needs of all the students in the classroom.

BIBLIOTHERAPY

WHAT IS BIBLIOTHERAPY?

Once in awhile a dramatic change occurs in the attitude or behavior of a student because of the influence of a special book. Learning about the similar experiences of others can provide hope and encouragement to students with special needs. Students with personal problems such as being overweight, too short, too tall, unpopular, or with academic or physical problems are sometimes able to identify with characters struggling with a similar circumstance. The right book can be a powerful influence to provide hope and motivation and improve social situations as well as academic learning situations. *Bibliotherapy* is a term given to the established practice of using books to help children solve personal problems. Bibliotherapy is based on the belief that through empathy with characters encountered in books, the reader becomes better able to understand him- or herself and his or her situation.

WHAT IS THE PURPOSE OF IMPLEMENTING BIBLIOTHERAPY?

The purpose of using bibliotherapy is to help the student learn more about him- or herself by searching an outside source. Teachers can use bibliotherapy to relieve conscious problems in a controlled manner for a specific student. It can also lead to an increase in understanding about human beings and human behavior.

WHEN SHOULD BIBLIOTHERAPY BE USED?

Bibliotherapy may be implemented for numerous reasons:

1. To help students enhance their concepts of self.
2. To increase understanding.
3. To foster realistic self-appraisal.
4. To find interests outside of oneself.
5. To relieve emotional pressures.
6. To promote the realization that the student is not the only one encountering a problem.
7. To recognize the fact that there is often more than one solution to a specific problem.
8. To become willing to discuss problems with freedom.
9. To help formulate an action plan.

Bibliotherapy requires careful planning and implementation. What techniques are recommended when sharing books with students? Whenever possible, teachers should implement these strategies when using bibliotherapy:

1. Listen carefully to the students. Be certain to observe body language and use eye contact. Teachers should paraphrase carefully what they think they hear the students saying. Be nonjudgmental and thank any student who shares thoughts or feelings.
2. Encourage the students to share thoughts and feelings. Help them explore those feelings and continue to be nonjudgmental.
3. Carefully prepare the students for a new class member, in particular a student with special needs. Read a book about the situation. Help the students determine how they will react to the new situation/student. If appropriate, practice role-playing situations.
4. Motivate the individual or individuals with preliminary activities prior to the book introduction.

5. Teachers should be sure to read the material carefully before sharing it with the students to ensure that it is appropriate for the classroom situation.
6. Allow time for students to absorb and reflect on the story.
7. Provide time for a follow-up discussion, art project, or journal entry.
8. Use strategic leading questions to invite students to empathize and relate to the book character's situation.
9. Conduct an assessment of the activity and provide for closure when possible.

WHAT ARE SOME SOURCES FOR FINDING QUALITY BOOKS FOR BIBLIOTHERAPY?

The teacher should look for books with literary merit that are well written and include high-quality illustrations, whenever possible. A few of the excellent resources for bibliotherapy selections follow:

- *More Notes from a Distant Drummer: A Guide to Juvenile Fiction Portraying the Disabled,* by B. H. Basken and K. H. Harris (1984)
- *Children's Literature in the Elementary School,* by C. S. Huck, S. Hepler, and J. Hickman (1997)
- *Books for Early Childhood: A Developmental Perspective,* edited by J. A. Pardeck and J. T. Pardeck (1986)
- *Portraying Persons with Disabilities: An Annotated Bibliography of Fiction for Children and Teenagers,* by D. E. J. Robertson (1992)

WHAT ARE SOME SPECIFIC BOOKS RECOMMENDED FOR USE IN BIBLIOTHERAPY WITH ELEMENTARY STUDENTS?

The following sampling of books has been used in the classroom and found to be effective with elementary students. Sometimes a book that has been in print for a number of years is the best example for a particular situation. Books are available for many additional topics such as the death of a grandparent, a divorce, and being overweight. Those listed here deal primarily with students having special needs in the elementary classroom. For additional books, research the book collections listed above or those at the local or school library.

Attention Deficit/Hyperactive Disorder (AD/HD)

- *Jumpin' Johnny Get Back to Work!: A Child's Guide to ADHD/Hyperactivity,* by Michael Gordon (1991)
- *Shelley, the Hyperactive Turtle,* by Deborah Moss (1989)

Down Syndrome

- *My Sister Is Different,* by Betty Ren Wright (1981)
- *Be Good to Eddie Lee,* by V. Fleming (1993)

Hearing

- *Mandy,* by Barbara D. Booth (1991)
- *Silent Lotus,* by Jeanne Lee (1991)

Learning Disabilities

- *Someone Special, Just Like You,* by T. Brown (1984)
- *Secrets Aren't (Always) for Keeps,* by B. Aiello and J. Shulman (1988)
- *Thank You, Mr. Falker,* by Patricia Polacco (1998)

Vision

- *Cromwell's Glasses,* by Holly Keller (1982)
- *Libby's New Glasses,* by Tricia Tusa (1984)

Wheelchair Use

- *Mama Zooms,* by Jane Cowan-Fletcher (1993)
- *A Very Special Critter,* by Gina Mayer and Mercer Mayer (1992)

Bibliotherapy provides the opportunity for teachers who love literature and reading to use that literature as a means to help students deal with the everyday problems of life and living. Through bibliotherapy students often can experience the feelings of others, be provided assistance in solving their own problems, gain understanding of the problems other people face, recognize that they are not alone in facing the problems, and discover new sources of information to assist them in making successful decisions. Bibliotherapy is an outstanding technique that can be used by teachers when working with students with and without special needs. Bibliotherapy promotes empathy and positive attitudes, encourages positive social skills and understanding, and instills a sense of respect for the needs of others.

BIBLIOGRAPHY

Aiello, B. & Shulman, J. (1988). *Secrets aren't (always) for keeps.* Breckenridge, CO: Twenty-first Century.

Armstrong, T. (1994). *Multiple intelligences in the classroom.* Alexandria, VA: ASCD.

Bandura, A. (1973). *Aggression: A social learning analysis.* Englewood Cliffs, NJ: Prentice-Hall.

Basken, B. H. & Harris, K. H. (1984). *More notes from a distant drummer: A guide to juvenile fiction portraying the disabled.* New York: Bowker.

Blanton, L. P., Griffin, C. C., Winn, J. A., & Pugach, M. C. (Eds.). (1997). *Teacher education in transition: Collaborative programs to prepare general and special educators.* Denver: Love.

Booth, B. D. (1991). *Mandy.* New York: Lothrop, Lee & Shephard.

Bos, C. S. & Vaughn, S. (Eds.). (1998). *Teaching students with learning and behavior problems.* 4th ed. Boston: Allyn & Bacon.

Bradley, D. F. & Calvin, M. B. (1998). Grading modified assignments: Equity or compromise? *Teaching Exceptional Children, 31,* no. 2, 24–29.

Brady, M. (1989). *What's worth teaching? Selecting, organizing and integrating knowledge.* New York: State University of New York Press.

Brett, A. (1998). Educational technology. In C. S. Bos & S. Vaughn (Eds.). *Strategies for teaching students with learning and behavior problems* (pp. 415–443). Boston: Allyn & Bacon.

Brooks, J. G. & Brooks, M. G. (1993). *In search of understanding: The case for constructivist classrooms.* Alexandria, VA: ASCD.

Brown, T. (1984). *Someone special, just like you.* New York: Holt, Rinehart & Winston.

Bryant, B. R. & Seay, P. C. (1998). Technology related assistance to individuals with disabilities act: Relevance to individuals with learning disabilities and their advocates. *Journal of Learning Disabilities, 31,* 4–15.

Bryant, D. P. & Bryant, B. R. (1998). Using assistive technology to include students with learning disabilities in cooperative learning activities. *Journal of Learning Disabilities, 31,* 41–54.

Bryant, D. P., Bryant, B. R., & Raskind, M. H. (1998). Using assistive technology to enhance the skills of students with learning disabilities. *Intervention in School and Clinic, 34,* no. 1 (September), 53–59.

Burke, M. D., Hagan, S. L., & Grossen, B. (1998). What curriculum designs and strategies accommodate diverse learners? *Teaching Exceptional Children* (September), 34–38, 85.

Bursuck, W., Polloway, E. A., Plante, L., Epstein, M. H., Jayanthis, M., & Coneghynd, M. C. (1996). Report card grading and adaptations: A national survey of classroom practices. *Exceptional Children, 62,* no. 4, 301–318.

Council for Exceptional Children. (1994). *Creating schools for all our students: What 12 schools have to say.* Reston, VA: Council for Exceptional Children.

Cowan-Fletcher, J. (1993). *Mama zooms.* New York: Scholastic.

Elias, M. J., Zins, J. E., Weissberg, R. P., Frey, K. S., Greenberg, M. T., Haynes, N. M., Kessler, R., Schwab-Stone, M. E., & Shriver, T. P. (1997). *Promoting social and emotional learning: Guidelines for educators.* Alexandria, VA: ASCD.

Finders, M. & Lewis, C. (1994). Why some parents don't come to school. *Educational Leadership, 51,* no. 8 (May), 50–54.

Finson, Kevin D. (Ed.). (1996). *Science in the mainstream: Retooling science assessment.* Macomb: Illinois State Board of Education Science Literacy Office.

Fleming, V. (1993). *Be good to Eddie Lee.* New York: Philomel.

Fosnot, C. T. (1996). Teachers construct constructivism: The center for constructivist teaching/teacher preparation project. In C. T. Fosnot (Ed.), *Constructivism: Theory, perspective, and practice* (pp. 205–216). New York: Teachers College Press.

Friend, M. & Bursuck, W. (1996). *Including students with special needs—A practical guide for classroom teachers.* Boston: Allyn & Bacon.

Fuchs, D., Fuchs, L., & Bahr, M. W. (1990). Mainstream assistance teams: A scientific basis for the art of consultation. *Exceptional Children, 57,* 128–139.

Gardner, H. (1983). *Frames of mind: The theory of multiple intelligences.* New York: Basic Books.

———. (1993). *Multiple intelligences: The theory into practice.* New York: Basic Books.

Gersten, R., Vaughn, S., & Brengleman, S. U. (1996). Grading and academic feedback for special education students and students with learning difficulties. In T. R. Guskey

(Ed.). *ASCD yearbook 1996: Communicating student learning* (pp. 47–57). Alexandria, VA: ASCD.

Getskow, V. & Konczal, D. (1996). *Kids with special needs: Information and activities to promote awareness and understanding.* Santa Barbara, CA: Learning Works.

Glatthorn, A. A. (1994). *Developing a quality curriculum.* Alexandria, VA: ASCD.

Gordon, M. (1991). *Jumpin' Johnny get back to work!: A child's guide to ADHD/hyperactivity.* Dewitt, NY: GSI.

Grenot-Scheyer, M., Jubala, K. A., Bishop, K. D., & Coots, J. J. (1996). *The inclusive classroom.* Westminster, CA: Teacher Created Materials.

Henley, M., Ramsey, R. S., & Algozzine, R. F. (2002). *Characteristics of and strategies for teaching students with mild disabilities.* 4th ed. Boston: Allyn & Bacon.

Holmes Group. (1986). *Tomorrow's teachers: A report of the Holmes Group.* East Lansing, MI: Holmes Group.

Huck, C. S., Hepler, S., & Hickman, J. (1997). *Children's literature in the elementary school.* New York: Holt, Rinehart & Winston.

Idol, L., Paolucci-Whitcomb, P., & Nevin, A. (1994). *Collaborative consultation.* 2d ed. Austin: Pro-Ed.

Individuals with Disabilities Education Act. (1999). Final rules and regulations. *Federal Register, 64,* no. 48 (March 12), 12239–12742.

Jacobs, H. H. (1989). *Interdisciplinary curriculum: Design and implementation.* Alexandria, VA: ASCD.

Kapusnick, R. A. & Hauslein, C. M. (2001). The "silver cup" of differentiated instruction. *Kappa Delta Pi Record, 37,* no. 4 (summer), 156–159.

Keller, H. (1982). *Cromwell's glasses.* Greenwillow.

Kellough, R. D. (1996). *Integrating math and science for intermediate and middle school students.* Englewood Cliffs, NJ: Prentice-Hall/Merrill.

Kirk, S. A., Gallagher, J. J., & Anastasiow, N. J. (2000). *Educating exceptional children.* Boston: Houghton Mifflin.

Kochhar, C. A. & West, L. L. (1996). *Handbook for successful inclusion.* Gaithersburg, MD: Aspen.

Kochhar, C. A., West, L. L., & Taymans, J. M. (2000). *Successful inclusion: Practical strategies for a shared responsibility.* Upper Saddle River, NJ: Prentice-Hall.

Kovalik, S. (1994). *ITI: The model.* 3d ed. Kent, WA: Books for Educators.

Lee, J. (1991). *Silent lotus.* New York: Farrar, Straus, & Giroux.

Lerner, J. W. (2000). *Learning disabilities: Theories, diagnosis, and teaching strategies.* Boston: Houghton Mifflin.

Lesar, S., Benner, S. M., Habel, J., & Coleman, L. (1997). Preparing general education teachers for inclusive settings: A constructivist teacher education program. *Teacher Education and Special Education, 20,* no. 3, 204–220.

Lewis, J. D. (1998). How the Internet expands educational options. *Teaching Exceptional Children, 30,* no. 5, 34–41.

Mayer, G. & Mayer, M. (1992). *A very special critter.* New York: Golden Books.

McCarty, H. & Chalmers, L. (1997). Bibliotherapy: Intervention and prevention. *Teaching Exceptional Children* (July–August), 12–17.

McGinnis, E. & Goldstein, A. P. (1997). *Skillstreaming the elementary school child.* Rev. ed. Champaign, IL: Research Press.

Moss, D. M. (1989). *Shelley, the hyperactive turtle.* Bethesda, MD: Woodbine House.

National Council of Teachers of Mathematics. (1989). *The curriculum and evaluation standards for school mathematics.* Reston, VA: NCTM.

————. (2000). *Principles and standards for school mathematics.* Reston, VA: NCTM.

National Research Council. (1995). *The national science education standards.* Washington, DC: National Academy Press.

Olson, J. L. & Platt, J. M. (1996). *Teaching children and adolescents with special needs.* Englewood Cliffs, NJ: Prentice-Hall.

O'Neil, J. (1994–95). Can inclusion work? A conversation. *Educational Leadership, 52,* no. 4 (December), 7–11.

Ornstein, A. C. & Behar-Horenstein, L. S. (1999). *Contemporary issues in curriculum.* 2d ed. Boston: Allyn & Bacon.

Ornstein, A. C. & Hunkins, F. P. (1998). *Curriculum: Foundations, principles and issues.* 3d ed. Boston: Allyn & Bacon.

Palmer, J. M. (1995). Interdisciplinary curriculum—again. In J. A. Beane (Ed.), *Toward a coherent curriculum* (pp. 55–56). Alexandria, VA: ASCD.

Pardeck, J. A. & Pardeck, J. T. (Eds.). (1986). *Books for early childhood: A developmental perspective.* New York: Greenwood.

Polacco, P. (1998). *Thank you, Mr. Falker.* New York: Philomel Books.

Pugach, M. C. & Johnson, L. J. (1993). *Collaborative practitioners, collaborative schools.* Denver: Love.

Raywid, M. (1993). Finding time for collaboration. *Educational Leadership, 51,* no. 1, 30–34.

Ring, M. M. (1997). Middle school accommodations and grading adjustments for students with learning disabilities. Paper presented at the meeting of the Council for Exceptional Children, Salt Lake City, April.

Robertson, D. E. J. (1992). *Portraying persons with disabilities: An annotated bibliography of fiction for children and teenagers.* New Providence, NJ: Bowker.

Ross, A. & Olsen, K. (1995). *A vision for the middle school through integrated thematic instruction.* 3d ed. Kent, WA: Books for Educators.

Sadker, M. P. & Sadker, D. M. (1997). *Teachers, schools, and society.* 4th ed. New York: McGraw-Hill.

Sapon-Shevin, M. (1994–95). Why gifted students belong in inclusive schools. *Educational Leadership, 52,* no. 4, 64–68, 70.

Sherry, L. & Spooner, F. (Eds.). (2000). *Unified teacher preparation programs for general and special educators.* St. Petersburg, FL: CSPD.

Smith, T., Polloway, E. A., Patton, J. R., & Dowdy, C. A. (1995). *Teaching students with special needs in inclusive settings.* Boston: Allyn & Bacon.

Stenmark, J. (Ed.). (1991). *Mathematics assessment: Myths, models, good questions, and practical suggestions.* Reston, VA: NCTM.

Stork, S. & Engel, S. (1999). So, what is constructivist teaching? A rubric for teacher education. *Dimensions of Early Childhood* (winter), 20–26.

Sugai, G. M. & Tindal, G. A. (1993). *Effective school consultation: An interactive approach.* Pacific Grove, CA: Brooks/Cole.

Tomlinson, C. A. (1999a). *The differentiated classroom: Responding to the needs of all learners.* Alexandria, VA: ASCD.

———. (1999b). Mapping a route toward differentiated instruction. *Educational Leadership, 57,* no. 1, 12–16.

Turnbull, A., Turnbull, R., Shank, M., Smith, S., & Leal, D. (2002). *Exceptional lives: Special education in today's schools.* 3d ed. Upper Saddle River, NJ: Merrill.

Tusa, T. (1984). *Libby's new glasses.* New York: Holiday House.

Vaughn, S., Bos, C. S., & Schumm, J. S. (2000). *Teaching exceptional, diverse, and at-risk students in the general education classroom.* 2d ed. Boston: Allyn & Bacon.

Vaughn, S. & La Greca, A. (1993). Social skills training: What, who, what and how. In W. N. Bender (Ed.), *Learning disabilities: Best practices for professionals* (pp. 251–271). North Potomac, MD: Andover Medical.

Villa, R. A. & Thousand, J. S. (Eds.). (1995). *Creating an inclusive school.* Alexandria, VA: ASCD.

Warger, C. D. & Pugach, M. C. (1996). Curriculum considerations in an inclusive environment. *Focus on Exceptional Children, 28,* no. 8, 1–12.

West, J. F., Idol, L., & Cannon, G. (1989). *Collaboration in the schools: An inservice and preservice curriculum for teachers, support staff, and administrators.* Austin: Pro-Ed.

Whittaker, C. R., Salend, S. J., & Duhaney, D. (2001). Creating instructional rubrics for inclusive classrooms. *Teaching Exceptional Children, 34,* no. 2 (November–December), 8–13.

Wigle, S. E. & Wilcox, D. J. (1996). Inclusion: Criteria for the preparation of education personnel. *Remedial and Special Education, 17,* no. 5, 323–328.

Winn, J. A. & Blanton, L. P. (1997). The call for collaboration in teacher education. In L. P. Blanton, C. C. Griffin, J. A. Winn, & M. C. Pugach (Eds.), *Teacher education in transition* (pp. 1–17). Denver: Love.

Wise, A. (1994). The coming revolution in teacher licensure: Redefining teacher preparation. *Action in Teacher Education, 16,* no. 2, 1–13.

Wright, B. R. (1981). *My sister is different.* Milwaukee: Raintree.

York, J. L. & Reynolds, M. C. (1996). Special education and inclusion. In J. Sikula, T. J. Buttery, & E. Guyton (Eds.), *Handbook of research on teacher education* (pp. 820–836). 2d ed. New York: Macmillan.

INDEX

ABOUT THE AUTHORS

Sally Cox Mayberry is a professor in the College of Education at Florida Gulf Coast University (FGCU). After receiving her undergraduate degree from Randolph-Macon Woman's College, she continued on to the University of Virginia to earn her master's degree. An elementary school teacher for fifteen years, she left the classroom to earn her doctorate at the University of Miami and enter the field of higher education. At FGCU, Mayberry teaches undergraduate and graduate classes in mathematics and science education as well as classroom management. Her current topics of interest are inclusion, problem solving, the integrated curriculum, critical thinking, authentic assessment, hands-on learning, and technology implementation.

A frequent presenter at national and state mathematics, science, and reading conferences, she is currently speaking on the integration of literature, mathematics, and science in the curriculum. Mayberry has authored and coauthored eight books and one article to date. Three additional articles are currently being reviewed. Entertaining a love for learning and teaching since she was a little girl, Mayberry still looks forward to her weekly visits to local schools, where she helps children learn firsthand about ladybugs, earthworms, and butterflies.

Brenda Belson Lazarus began her teaching career in general education classrooms at the elementary and junior high school levels. She became interested in working with students with learning and behavior differences while teaching students who were labeled "at risk" and "remedial." She went on to study special education and taught at the middle school, high school, and elementary school levels. Lazarus taught for twelve years before becoming a university teacher educator. She taught at Grand Valley State University from 1985 to 1997 and has been a professor at Florida Gulf Coast University since the college was founded in 1997. Lazarus teaches undergraduate and graduate courses in special education methods, classroom management, and human diversity.

Lazarus obtained her bachelor's degree from Albion College (Mich.), a master's degree in elementary education with an emphasis in reading from Wayne State University, a master's degree in special education from Oakland University, and a doctorate in philosophy in 1985 from Michigan State University. Her areas of interest are inclusion, case study methodology, distance learning delivery, and integrated teacher education programs.